Gavin Weightman is the author of a series of colourful history books including *The Frozen Water Trade*, *Signor Marconi's Magic Box*, *The Industrial Revolutionaries*, and *Children of Light: How Electricity Changed Britain Forever*.

After taking a degree in sociology at London University Gavin joined the staff of *New Society* in the mid-1970s as a feature writer. In 1978 he was recruited by London Weekend Television to produce and direct documentaries. These included two six-part history series entitled The Making of Modern London, as well as City Safari, Brave New Wilderness, London River and Bright Lights, Big City. For two years he was the presenter of The London Programme on LWT.

He has published more than twenty books and written for numerous publications including *History Today*, the *Guardian*, the *Sunday Times* and the *Independent*. In 2012 the Royal Literary Fund appointed him as a Fellow at Queen Mary College, University of London.

He lives in Highbury, North London with illustrator Clare Beaton.

You can find him at:

www.gavin-weightman.co.uk

Also by Gavin Weightman

Signor Marconi's Magic Box
'Gavin Weightman brings alive the excitement and uncertainty of the early wireless experiments…an excellent read' *New Scientist*

'fascinating' *New York Times Book Review*

'most entertaining and difficult to put down.' *Irish Examiner*

Children of Light
'brisk and entertaining…lucid and fascinating' *Sunday Times*

'Highly recommended' *Readers Digest*

The Industrial Revolutionaries
'Weightman is excellent at demolishing some of the myths of the industrial revolution' *Literary Review*

London River: A History of the Thames
'The Thames has attracted many authors…best, by far, Gavin Weightman, *London River*' Roy Porter in *London: A Social History*

The Frozen Water Trade
'Weightman… creates a funny, rollicking human adventure' *Publishers Weekly*

A brisk delightful history' *National Geographic Adventure*

'An entertaining history'*The New Yorker*

'Splendid…a page turner, gripping in its saga, epic in its implications' *Dallas Morning News*

The Making of Modern London: A people's history
'A brilliant account… What a satisfying blend of meticulous research and human stories' BBC *Who Do You Think You Are?* Magazine (book co-authored with S. Humphries)

Secrets of a Titanic Victim

The story of the real *My Fair Lady*

Gavin Weightman

backstory

First published in 2012 by Backstory
info@backstory.la

Copyright © Gavin Weightman

The moral right of the author of this work has been asserted by him in accordance with the Copyright, Designs and Patents Act of 1988.

All rights reserved.
No part of this book may be reproduced, stored or transmitted in any form or bay any means without the prior permission of both the copyright owner and the publisher of this book.

A CIP catalogue for this book is available from the British Library.

ISBN: 978-0-9562462-1-9

www.backstory.la

Acknowledgements

Over the years that I have studied the case of Eliza Armstrong I have been in touch with many people who have been generous with their time and knowledge. For the whole of the period of my research, Owen Mulpetre, creator of the W. T. Stead resource site, has provided both insight and valuable help with sources and material.

I am indebted to Alan Andrews, formerly Professor of History at Dalhousie University, Nova Scotia, who put me in touch with the work of Celia Marshik on Shaw's parody of Stead's "stunt" in *Pygmalion*. Essex Record Office did their best to help me in my search for the later life of Eliza Armstrong. Most of my collection of newspaper cuttings, in particular those from *Lloyd's Weekly Illustrated Newspaper* were collected diligently by Patrick McDonnell at the British Newspaper Library in Colindale. Pamela Walker, author of an excellent history of the Salvation Army, gave me some very helpful background on Rebecca Jarrett. The Salvation Army's own archive also gave me willing assistance.

As always, the collections of the British Library were invaluable and the staff of the London Library have been very helpful. I would like to thank Brian Stewart, Distinguished Senior Fellow at the Munk School of Global Affairs in Toronto for his very helpful comments on the text, though responsibility for what is published here is mine. Finally, I would like to thank Ralph Jones for making publication of this book possible through the newly created imprint Backstory.

CONTENTS

Dramatis Personae	9
Forward	13
1 Read all about it	18
2 A mother seeking a lost child	29
3 A Victorian slum	35
4 'A child of thirteen bought for £5'	44
5 The mystery of Hope Cottage	51
6 The Mansion House Committee	56
7 Anger in Charles Street	61
8 A letter from Eliza	68
9 Eliza's return	74
10 The long arm of the law	80
11 Eliza tells her story	91
12 The drunken mother of Charles Street	98
13 Revelations at the Old Bailey	110
14 The judge and the jury	126
15 The joy of prison	131
16 Still lying about Eliza	136
17 The aftermath	140

18 The white slave trade	149
19 The deal	157
20 Eliza immortalised	161
21 Stead: In memoriam	166
Timeline	169
A note on sources	173
Select bibliography	174

Dramatis Personae

W. T. Stead and Eliza Armstrong

William Thomas Stead, always known as W. T. Stead (1849-1912), editor of the London evening newspaper the *Pall Mall Gazette*

Eliza Armstrong, aged thirteen, who became the playwright George Bernard Shaw's model for Eliza Doolittle.

Elizabeth Armstrong and Charles Armstrong

Charles Armstrong, Eliza's father, a chimney sweep who bore some resemblance to Shaw's creation, Alfred P. Doolittle.

Elizabeth Armstrong, Eliza's mother who is accused of selling her daughter to a brothel keeper.

Rebecca Jarrett and Nancy Broughton

Rebecca Jarrett, former prostitute and brothel keeper, who was instructed by Stead to go out and buy girls to provide evidence for his investigation into vice in London. Born around 1850 she later worked for the Salvation Army.

Nancy Broughton, neighbour of the Armstrong family in Lisson Grove and a friend of Rebecca Jarrett who introduced her to Eliza Armstrong. Nancy and Rebecca had met when they both worked at Claridge's.

Jack 'Bash' Broughton, Nancy's husband.

Katie Booth sister of Bramwell and pioneer of French Salvation Army in Paris where she was known as La Marechale.

Inspector Edward Borner, Scotland Yard officer charged by the Marylebone Magistrates with finding Eliza. He was the one who tracked her down.

Thomas Catling, Editor of *Lloyd's Weekly Illustrated Newspaper* who befriended and aided the Armstrong family.

Thomas Edwards, manager of a women's refuge near the Armstrong's home who knew Jarrett, and her history as a brothel keeper, and helped Mrs Armstrong in her struggles to get her daughter back.

Bramwell Booth and Samson Jacques

Bramwell Booth, son of the founders of the Salvation Army, was Chief of Staff of that organisation in 1885. He was charged with abduction and acquitted at the Old Bailey.

Sampson Jacques (alias Mr Mussabini) journalist recruited by Stead to show him around London's brothels and to provide him with the contacts to mimic the ruination of young girls.

Madame Mourez and Madame Combe

Madame Mourez, elderly French midwife and alleged abortionist. Uniquely among the defendants, she was charged with a felony rather than a misdemeanour. (Sometimes spelt Mourey.)

Madame Combe, Salvation Army member, recruited by Bramwell Booth for his part in the Maiden Tribute scandal. She was tried and acquitted. (Sometimes spelt Coombe.)

Dr Heywood Smith and Harry Bodkin Poland Q.C.

Dr Heywood Smith, whose involvement with Stead almost wrecked his career as a leading gynaecologist in London.

Harry Bodkin Poland, chief prosecuting counsel at Bow Street Magistrates Court, who created a fund to provide help for the Armstrong family.

George Bernard Shaw, who wrote book reviews for the *Pall Mall Gazette* in 1885 and was finishing his final draft of *Pygmalion* in the summer of 1912, when much was written about Stead after his death on the Titanic.

Forward

It was my interest in very early wireless telegraphy which led me to the Titanic disaster and a re-acquaintance with one of those who perished in the early hours of Monday 15 April 1912. Using Morse Code, two young Marconi operators tapped out the shocking message that the liner had hit an iceberg and was sinking. It was late at night and touch and go if any other ships picked up the distress signal. By chance a Marconi telegrapher on another ship in the Atlantic, the Carpathia, heard the signal as he was about to go to bed. He tapped out to the operators on the Titanic: 'Do you know Cape Race has messages for you?' He got the reply: 'Come at once, we have struck a berg. Its a CQD OM'. This message, using Marconi's own distress signal CQD (the OM was the sign-off all Marconi men used, meaning Old Man) brought the Carpathia to the scene of the disaster in time to save 712 lives.

Rescue came too late for 1514 who died in the icy waters. Among these victims were many wealthy and famous people travelling first class on this most luxurious of Atlantic liners. When I re-visited the tragedy while researching my book *Signor Marconi's Magic Box* one celebrated name in particular caught my attention: W. T. Stead.

A long while back the exploits of Stead when he was editor of the London evening newspaper the *Pall Mall Gazette* had been touched on in a course I had taken in social history which included what was called "The New Journalism" of the late Victorian period. Stead's special notoriety arose from a sensational stunt in which he claimed he had personally witnessed the purchase of a young girl and her sale to a brothel for the sum of £5. The sale of children into prostitution in London, Stead had claimed, was rife and he took the risk of ending up in jail himself in order to demonstrate how easy it was to buy and sell virgins in the very heart of the British Empire.

That was all I could remember of the story, though I had a glancing acquaintance with it now and again over a period of thirty years or so for it is recounted casually in a great many books, and dealt with in more detail in just one or two. When I was reminded that Stead had gone down with the Titanic my interest in his story was rekindled and I began to discover very quickly that it was far more controversial than I had imagined. Most of the potted histories of Stead's "£5 virgin" stunt were wildly inaccurate. My research took me from the obituaries of Stead written at the time of his death—these were published world wide as he had an international reputation—back to original sources.

I was fortunate as I delved deeper into the story that the Internet had begun to offer the lone author working at home with a computer a wealth of original material. This included Victorian newspapers which I could access and read on-line, as well as many magazine articles.

And, most stimulating of all, I was directed to a website which had the intriguing address of 'attacking the devil' (www.attackingthedevil.co.uk). It was the creation of a post-graduate student, Owen Mulpetre, who was working on a doctorate on The New Journalism, with Stead as his central focus of interest. In order to gather information he learned to create a website which in turn was immensely helpful to me. Owen's web address was taken from Stead's exclamation when, at the tender age of twenty-two, he first had the opportunity to edit a newspaper, the *Northern Echo*: "What a wonderful way of attacking the devil!".

That battle cry gives some measure of the man. Of medium height, with a thick red beard, Stead had a messianic, almost crazy demeanour and for most of his life appears to have been in a state of moral agitation and excitement. Certainly, by his own account, he was in a state of almost euphoric zeal when he observed the reaction to the publication in July 1885 of the first instalment of the *Pall Mall Gazette*'s portentously titled investigation into prostitution in London, The Maiden Tribute to Modern Babylon. He watched as newspaper boys scrambled to claim their copies and headed out into the streets with column inches which would horrify his readers in the Victorian suburbs.

The *Gazette*'s lurid account of vice in the capital was published anonymously, the author signing himself the Chief Director of the Secret Commission. Stead hid behind this puerile disguise for a while just as he had ventured into the brothels and 'gay houses' of Victorian London comically disguised as 'an American tourist'. Nearly all the evidence he offered the reader was hearsay. Nobody was named. It was the anonymous bragging of countless pimps, prostitutes and brothel keepers with some opinions of an un-named senior policeman. It might all have been dismissed as unverifiable if it had not been for one story headlined

"A girl of thirteen bought for £5"

This could not be branded as just another unsubstantiated story from London's underworld. The "Chief Director" assured readers of the *Gazette* that he could vouch personally for the truth of it in every detail. Exactly how was not made clear. But the story of the purchase and subsequent vetting and sale of the virgin was given in some detail. Even a description of the girl herself and of her family. In a bathetic finale the little victim was heard to plead: "Take me home, take me home!"

In time, Stead's audacious claims were to pass into journalistic legend for his Maiden Tribute campaign had a profound political and moral purpose: it was not mere sensationalism. There is little doubt that it was Stead's report which succeeded in shocking Parliament into passing a new law to protect young girls from abduction and violation. The month after the publication of the Maiden Tribute investigation and the story of the "£5 virgin", the Criminal Law Amendment Act raised the age of consent for girls from thirteen to sixteen, where it remains to this day.

However, not long after the change in the law and the triumphant celebrations of Stead's achievement, a story began to unfold which was to cause him and those who backed him acute embarrassment. Just about everything in his supposedly irrefutable story of the purchase of the girl of thirteen was either fabricated or inaccurate.

The true story of the £5 virgin is what this book is about and it is, in my view, a quite shocking indictment of Stead's journalistic methods which were both duplicitous and callous. While researching the story in depth, I discovered, to my great satisfaction, that I had an ally in the playwright George Bernard Shaw. An account of how Shaw borrowed much of the detail of Stead's £5 virgin story to create Eliza Doolittle, star of his play *Pygmalion*, which later became the musical *My Fair Lady*, is told towards the end of this book. Although he first conceived of the play fifteen years earlier, Shaw was putting the finishing touches to the script when the Titanic went down. It brought back to him the events of 1885 which were still sharp in his memory for he had been a book reviewer for the *Pall Mall Gazette* when the Maiden Tribute stories were published.

Shaw supported Stead until he discovered to his disgust that the whole £5 virgin story was, as he told Stead's biographer, a "put up job" which Stead himself had "put up." A parody of Stead's great 'scoop' plays a large part in the plot and text of *Pygmalion* and the little girl that Stead supposedly bought is, in so many ways, the model for Shaw's eternally popular heroine Eliza Doolittle.

Certainly the playwright lost all respect for Stead for he gave a damning judgement on him after a few years after the Titanic disaster: "He had, as far as I could see, no general knowledge of art or history, philosophy or science, with which to co-ordinate his journalistic discoveries; and it was consequently impossible for cultured minds to get into any sort of effective contact with him except on the crudest common ground. This is the explanation of his ineffectiveness for anything wider and deeper than a journalistic stunt."

Nevertheless, Stead remained obdurate in his defence of what he did and immensely proud of his exploits. He said he would be happy to have "the man who wrote the Maiden Tribute" as his epitaph. But he never provided posterity with a true account of what happened when he claimed he had bought a virgin from her mother, taken her to a brothel, and then 'rescued' her. All the versions he wrote subsequently omit the most embarrassing aspects of his exploits. However, these are recorded in newspaper reports and court records available to the historian. *Secrets of a Titanic victim: the story of the real My Fair Lady* draws on this extensive archive to put the record straight.

The true story of a real life Eliza Doolittle did not perish with the Titanic.

Gavin Weightman
Highbury
January, 2012

Chapter One
Read all about it

Though Stead later protested that the story of the girl bought for £5 was really inconsequential, and that he nearly left it out, that was not the view of the boys who set out to make a penny or two hawking the *Pall Mall Gazette* on the streets of London that summer evening on 6 July 1885. I cannot imagine that they patiently read the whole of the first long-winded instalment and picked out the story of the girl 'Lily' whose virginity was sacrificed to the London Minotaurs.

Someone on the *Gazette* must have directed them to that item, for it was the headline of their hastily written billboards and placards. They were having a field day because the largest newsagent, W. H. Smith, which had the franchise at all the main railway stations, had refused to sell the *Gazette* as it regarded the Maiden Tribute investigation as obscene.

Something of the outrage that the sale of these editions of the newspaper gave rise to on the streets of the capital that evening can be gathered from a letter to the *Law Quarterly Review* written by a Mr Phillips, a member of the Bengal Civil Service who happened to be on leave in London:

" '£5 FOR A VIRGIN WARRANTED PURE!' is a specimen of the placards exhibited in the streets" he wrote. "I can vouch for the truth of the following occurrence. Two modest young girls of about fifteen were waiting for an omnibus outside Charing Cross Station. Their eyes being attracted by the huge placards and pictures of, or in imitation of the *Pall Mall Gazette*, one of the hawkers cried out: 'Come on Miss, 'ave a copy. This'll show you 'ow to earn five pounds!' Such a remark, made to a woman in India, would be punishable with one year's imprisonment and fine."

It is a scene that might easily have found a place in one of Shaw's plays, the respectable population of clerks and stockbrokers, seamstresses and maids, harangued by an army of artful dodgers as they made their way home to the newly built suburbs of Muswell Hill or Wimbledon. They were certainly Stead's intended audience and he had warned them in previous editions of the *Gazette* that they would be in for a shock if they chose to read his exposé of vice in the capital.

"We have no desire to inflict upon unwilling eyes the ghastly story of the criminal developments of modern vice," intoned the previous Saturday's editorial. "Therefore we say quite frankly to-day that all those who are squeamish, and all those who are prudish, and all those who prefer to live in a fool's paradise of imaginary innocence and purity, selfishly oblivious to the horrible realities which torment those whose lives are passed in the London Inferno, will do well not to read the Pall Mall Gazette of Monday and the three following days. The story of an actual pilgrimage into a real hell is not pleasant reading, and is not meant to be. It is, however, an authentic record of unimpeachable facts, 'abominable, unutterable, and worse than fables yet have feigned or fear conceived.' But it is true, and its publication is necessary."

The ban by W. H. Smith had been anticipated and the *Gazette* had taken the precaution of recruiting newsboys to hawk that evening's edition around the capital. Nudging each other, laughing and joking, and excited by the promise of a few pence profit from their sales, the boys formed a scrum outside the *Gazette* offices in Northumberland Street, then dashed off into the streets before they had had time to know what it was all about. But they had their headline, their cry:

"£5 a virgin, virgins for £5"

It took some time for tired eyes to find the reference in the *Gazette* to the "£5 virgin" for the revelations entitled The Maiden Tribute to Modern Babylon began in mock gothic style with an account of the sacrificial tribute of young girls and boys made by Athenians who sent them to the labyrinths to be deflowered and devoured by the Minotaur. It transpired that the investigation by something called the Secret Commission had identified in "Modern Babylon", that is to say, London, monsters as grotesque as the mythical Minotaur, and that not a few of them were the very gentlemen clutching the *Gazette* with growing rage on their way back to genteel homes.

It was the uncontrolled lust of wealthy men for young girls, preferably virgins, which was satisfied in the sexual market place by the wiles of evil women who procured a constant supply of maidens. Once enticed from their homes or from the drudgery of their work as governesses, nurses or servants there was no way back from the London labyrinth for these girls.

"This very night in London, and every night, year in and year out, not seven maidens only, but many times seven, selected almost as much by chance as those who in the Athenian market-place drew lots as to which should be flung into the Cretan labyrinth, will be offered up as the Maiden Tribute of Modern Babylon. Maidens they were when this morning dawned, but to-night their ruin will be accomplished, and to-morrow they will find themselves within the portals of the maze of London brotheldom. Within that labyrinth wander, like lost souls, the vast host of London prostitutes, whose numbers no man can compute, but who are probably not much below 50,000 strong. Many, no doubt, who venture but a little way within the maze make their escape. But multitudes are swept irresistibly on and on to be destroyed in due season, to give place to others, who also will share their doom.

The maw of the London Minotaur is insatiable, and none that go into the secret recesses of his lair return again."

Readers of the *Gazette* were required to plough through this purple prose for a considerable depth of column inches before they came to the raw, saucy bits which made eyes stand out on stalks and must have misted up many a polite pince-nez. Then the author of the piece began to hit home. There was an interview with a 'reformed', or possibly just 'retired' brothel keeper from the Mile End Road in East London written out apparently verbatim. His revelations read more like a boast than a confessional:

"Many women who are on the streets have female children. They are worth keeping. When they get to be twelve or thirteen they become merchantable. For a very likely 'mark' of this kind you may get as much as £20 or £40. I sent my own daughter out on the streets from my own brothel. I know a couple of very fine little girls now who will be sold before very long. They are bred and trained for the life. They must take the first step some time, and it is bad business not to make as much out of that as possible. Drunken parents often sell their children to brothel keepers. In the East-end, you can always pick up as many fresh girls as you want. In one street in Dalston you might buy a dozen. Sometimes the supply is in excess of the demand, and you have to seduce your maid yourself, or to employ some one else to do it, which is bad business in a double sense."

The Chief Director, anxious to test the authenticity of this wicked informant's claims asked him to supply him with some girls. For one reason or another the trade fell through and no girls appeared. However another trader in young girls came forward and, out of shame at her past life, agreed to provide an account of how the business was done. This woman, a seasoned 'procuress' and keeper of 'gay' houses was apparently reformed and known to the Chief Director through contacts who could vouch for her honesty.

She told him:

"Pretty girls who are poor, and who have either no parents or are away from home, are easiest picked up. How is it done? You or your decoy find a likely girl, and then you track her down. I remember I once went a hundred miles and more to pick up a girl. I took a lodging close to the board school, where I could see the girls go backwards and forwards every day. I soon saw one that suited my fancy. She was a girl of about thirteen, tall and forward for her age, pretty, and likely to bring business. I found out she lived with her mother. I engaged her to be my little maid at the lodgings where I was staying. The very next day I took her off with me to London and her mother never saw her again.

What became of her? A gentleman paid me £13 for the first of her, soon after she came to town. She was asleep when he did it—sound asleep. To tell the truth, she was drugged. It is often done. I gave her a drowse. It is a mixture of laudanum and something else. Sometimes chloroform is used, but I always used either snuff or laudanum. We call it drowse or black draught, and they lie almost as if dead, and the girl never knows what has happened till morning. And then? Oh! then she cries a great deal from pain, but she is 'mazed, and hardly knows what has happened except that she can hardly move from pain. Of course we tell her it is all right; all girls have to go through it some time, that she is through it now without knowing it, and that it is no use crying. It will never be undone for all the crying in the world. She must now do as the others do. She can live like a lady, do as she pleases, have the best of all that is going, and enjoy herself all day."

Once again, the Chief Director asked for a girl to be procured on his behalf. However, at the last minute she 'escaped'. While pursuing his investigation he chanced upon an aspect of the trade which he found particularly ghastly.

> "This was nothing less than the unearthing of a house, kept apparently by a highly respectable midwife, where children were taken by procurers to be certified as virgins before violation, and where, after violation, they were taken to be 'patched up', and where, if necessary, abortion could be procured. The existence of the house was no secret. It was well known in the trade, and my agent was directed thither without much ado by a gay woman with whom he had made a casual acquaintance. No doubt the respectable old lady has other business of a less doubtful character, but in the trade her repute is unrivalled, first as a certificator of virginity, and secondly for the adroitness and skill with which she can repair the laceration caused by the subsequent outrage."

The cries of London's sacrificial maidens were not heeded, said the Chief Director, for they were violated, drugged and sometimes flogged in dungeon rooms from which no sounds could be heard. The law turned a blind eye, and the police were in any case powerless to do anything. What was needed was a change in the law, the very piece of legislation which Parliament had dithered over for years despite the desperate pleas of thousands of campaigners. The age of sexual consent was then just thirteen: it must be raised to sixteen or eighteen.

A Criminal Law Amendment Bill which would do that and much more to protect young girls from vice was before Parliament at that very time but the House of Commons refused to pass it. The Maiden Tribute of Modern Babylon was written to shock MPs out of their complacency. And if all the evidence gathered by the

Chief Director and his Secret Commission from London's sexual underworld was not enough, then perhaps they would like to contemplate the following revelation. The 'Commission' had acted out the role of London Minotaur and had bought themselves a little virgin of their own. She had cost them £5, about £420 in today's money. This claim was truly sensational and provided the *Gazette* with its Monday night headlines.

Over the next few days, the correspondence columns of the newspapers burned with rage: was the *Gazette* not teaching young people how to enter the lucrative trade of prostitution?

A letter to St James's *Gazette*, headed "Champions of Innocence", complained that youngsters aged thirteen to fifteen from the Kensington House Boys Brigade had been recruited to sell "a certain foul publication on Monday night." While the publishers of the *Pall Mall Gazette* pretended to be on the side of virtue and to be wild with indignation at the debauchery of the poor man's children, they did not "scruple to put their unutterably obscene revelations into the hands of these helpless boys, not only to read, but to make a profit by selling it."

A response came quickly from the man in charge of Boys Brigade: he had been asked to supply his lads to distribute editions of the *Gazette* which he had been led to understand would "help legislation for the protection of young girls". When the last boy had rushed off with Monday night's copy he had looked at the newspaper for the first time and immediately went in pursuit. He had, in short, been duped and would never have offered the boys in his care as sellers if he had known the nature of the material printed in the paper.

In the City of London, the police rounded up the newspaper boys who were charged with causing an obstruction. The magistrates considered prosecuting them for distributing obscene material, although that appeared to be far-fetched. In Parliament the Home Secretary was asked if he would not ban the newspaper which was intent on publishing further revelations over the next three nights, but no action was taken. The newspaper's editor, W. T. Stead was asked to withdraw the articles voluntarily but he refused. He said he would only do so if Parliament put through the Criminal Law Amendment Bill which would raised the existing age of sexual consent for young girls from thirteen to sixteen. That was, after all, the purpose of the Maiden Tribute articles. When no assurance was forthcoming, the *Gazette* continued to publish its revelations.

Tuesday evening's edition had the following bathetic account of the nature of the virgin sacrifice:

> "Now it is a fact which I have repeatedly verified that girls of thirteen, fourteen, and even fifteen, who profess themselves perfectly willing to be seduced, are absolutely and totally ignorant of the nature of the act to which they assent. I do not mean merely its remoter consequences and the extent to which their consent will prejudice the whole of their future life, but even the mere physical nature of the act to which they are legally competent to consent is unknown to them. Perhaps one of the most touching instances of this and the most conclusive was the exclamation of relief that burst from a Birmingham girl of fourteen when the midwife had finished her examination.
>
> 'It's all over now,' she said, 'I am so glad.'
>
> 'You silly child,' said the procuress, 'that's nothing. You've not been seduced yet. That is still to come.'"

One tale after another of seduction was given in full. The Chief Director continued to recount incidents in which he had ordered up girls for £20. He believed the 'wholesale' price for virgins was £5, the East End price around £10 and the West End price £20. He provided 'evidence' that he had been able to get certificates verifying the virginity of a number of girls. He gave accounts of girls as young as five being violated, not as prostitutes but by paedophiles, some of whom had been convicted and sentenced to penal servitude.

By the time of the publication of the third instalment of the Maiden Tribute investigation, a huge crowd of newspaper boys anxious to get the paper before the print run ran out, as well as Londoners angered by the story, besieged the *Gazette*'s offices in Northumberland Street. Fights began and the windows of the newspaper offices were smashed. The *Gazette* itself wrote up the story as "The Siege of Northumberland Street".

> "For three days the crowd of hungry runners have surged down upon us. Gaunt, hollow-faced men and women, with trailing dress and ragged coats. Like others in Lombard-street and Capel-court, they fought for profit, buying in a cheap market to sell in a dear one. Neither better nor worse. London is raging for news and sends its regiments for the supply. And so the crowd raged at the door under the summer sky— raged and wrestled, fought with fist and feet, with tooth and nail, clamouring for the sheets wet from the press, a sea of human faces, tossed hither and thither by the resistless tide which swept from the Strand above; gesticulating, unceasingly hooting, groaning, climbing on window-sill, taking refuge on doorsteps. It brought its food and waited its turn till minutes grew to hours.
>
> Now and then there was a break, but it dosed up again like the tide over a drowning man. Artists came with their books, reporters from a friendly press, and candid friends in broad cloth with mouths agape. And the surging force grew in numbers and battled at the doors like troops of devils. The office under lock and key. Every door was barricaded. Only night intervened. At noon yesterday the arm of the law was requisitioned and responded. Four of the most

stalwart of the police marched down from Bow-street —at their head an officer. The three doors of entry to the office were under guard. An hour passed and the howling vendors were passed in for fresh supplies by regiments of twelve. The process was too slow. At one the window smashing began. The windows of machine-room, the windows of publishing office fell. Demands for reinforcements to Bow-street and Scotland-yard, quickly responded to by a more formidable band of forty more men of the force, acting under the direction of Superintendent Thompson, famous in the annals of the police, and alert for fame."

And this was not just a London news story. As the *Gazette* was proud to inform its readers, the Maiden Tribute revelations were telegraphed around the world. Pirate copies were soon being sold in America, and newsboys there were arrested as they had been in the City of London. Respectable newspapers, like the *New York Herald*, expressed disgust at the publication of such obscene material which it described as "sewage". Around the world there was widespread condemnation of what the *Gazette* had dared to put into print. But at home the Maiden Tribute re-kindled a moral purity campaign which had burned out in the 1880s. Meetings were called around the country urging the government to push through the Criminal Law Amendment Bill and the pressure to do so became irresistible. It was given a second reading and was heading for the statute books by the end of July.

The *Gazette*, its Secret Commission and its Chief Director were triumphant. No prosecution was brought for publishing obscene material and, as far as the law was concerned, they were apparently in the clear. There was just one episode in the investigation which could now get them into trouble.

The Chief Director, whom everyone now knew to be the *Gazette*'s editor, William Thomas Stead, had made a claim which suggested that he had personally been involved in the purchase of a thirteen year old girl. Under the sub-heading: "A child of thirteen bought for five pounds" the Chief Director had written: "Let me conclude the chapter of horrors by one incident, and only one of those which are constantly occurring in those dread regions of subterranean vice in which sexual crime flourishes almost unchecked. I can personally vouch for the absolute accuracy of every fact in the narrative."

Could the girl he called 'Lily' be real and the victim of a callous transaction which involved a verification of her virginity at the hands of an abortionist? Surely she was just another figment of Stead's lurid and licentious imagination. Whether she was or not, Stead himself seemed confident that he would be able to preserve her anonymity just as he had that of the whole gruesome cast who played a part in the sacrificial world of Modern Babylon.

Chapter Two
A mother seeking a lost child

In 1885, London was the largest and most exciting city in the industrialised world, the heart of a great empire, teeming with people from the very wealthiest to the most destitute. There was a huge working class population and literally thousands of street urchins and orphans. If a child should go missing in this metropolis it would hardly be news. When, therefore, the most popular Sunday newspaper of the day, *Lloyd's Weekly Illustrated,* printed on 12 July a story headlined "A Mother Seeking her lost child" there was bound to be more to it than met the eye.

Someone had tipped off the newly appointed editor, Thomas Catling, that rumours in the desperately impoverished enclave where this mother lived suggested there might be some link between the disappearance of her daughter and the recent revelations in the *Pall Mall Gazette.* Certainly, a man who ran one of the many rescue missions nearby, and was familiar with the prostitutes in the area, had been aware that a notorious brothel keeper and procuress, very like the un-named informant in the Maiden Tribute story, had been spotted locally. *Lloyd's Weekly* sent a reporter to investigate. This was his report:

"Yesterday, at Marylebone police-court, a poor but apparently respectable woman, renewed an application to Mr. Cooke for his advice in regard to her daughter, whom she said she had not seen or heard of since last May. A neighbour, she informed the magistrate, asked her if she would like her daughter to go out to service, and that if she did she knew of a very nice situation. She was spoken to, and after some consultation the applicant was persuaded to consent to the girl going to the place, which was said to be at Croydon; the only condition being that an opportunity should be given to her daughter, who was a fairly good scholar, to write home to her parents once a week.

She left home to go to the lady at Croydon on Derby Day, and the applicant had not heard tidings of her daughter since. Her neighbour had stated that she had received a letter from the girl's mistress and a sovereign, and that her daughter was quite well, but when she (the applicant) wrote to her daughter at the address given, which was Manchester, the letter was returned by the post officials as 'not known'. When asked how it was that the girl should be at Manchester when it was clearly understood that she was to live at Croydon, her neighbour said that the girl's master was a commercial traveller, and moved about a good deal. (The applicant at this point wept bitterly, and in broken sentences and with a faltering voice said her dear girl was only 13 years of age and she feared some harm had happened to her).

Mr Cooke: 'Do you mean to say you let the girl go away with strangers without making further enquiry than what you have just explained?'

Applicant: 'Well, Sir, she said, I should hear from her every week.'

Mr Cooke: 'Then I consider it a very great negligence on your part. You know you are the mother of that girl, and that she is underage.'

By the direction of the magistrate Sergeant Carden, who is the chief warrant officer, made further enquiries into the matter, and subsequently reported that he ascertained that the woman *(ie the one who had taken the girl)* ...had been at one time a fellow servant of the applicant's neighbour; that she had been in an infirmary; that the charity organisation society had helped her into a situation: and that she had since got married. The reason for the letter being returned to the post office was that it had been addressed to a place near Manchester instead of a place near Winchester.

The matter was still unsatisfactory, for the applicant's neighbours did not know where the girl went to, except that it was somewhere near Croydon. Mr Cooke directed that the matter should be further inquired into."

Meanwhile, *Lloyd's Weekly* began its own investigation. The mother in search of her child was a Mrs Elizabeth Armstrong who lived at 32 Charles Street, Lisson Grove. Her missing daughter was called Eliza and had been taken away by a woman friendly with a neighbour in Charles Street who lived at No. 37. This was Nancy Broughton who lived in one room with her husband, known as 'Bash', who was a local handyman working for a Marylebone housing association. The reporter was ushered in by the Broughton's and found the "room hung round with scenes illustrating the stations of the cross, and the walls decorated with crucifixes and portraits of popes and cardinals."

Since the publication of the story of the "girl of thirteen bought for £5" rumours had arisen in Charles Street that the girl the *Gazette* had called Lily was, in reality, Mrs Armstrong's daughter Eliza. If that was the case then Mrs Broughton and Bash were implicated in a most iniquitous transaction as it was she who had introduced Mrs Armstrong to her friend who had disappeared with Eliza. The *Lloyd's Weekly* reporter found the couple in a very agitated state. Mrs Armstrong had called Nancy a "bloody cow" and had accused her of being a brothel-keeper. The woman who had taken away Mrs Armstrong's daughter was a friend of hers, a Rebecca Jarrett known to her affectionately as Becky. They had met two years before when they both worked in the laundry at Claridge's Hotel.

31

Nancy had helped Becky out when she injured her hip "falling through a skylight". The reporter was shown letters Becky had written to Nancy thanking her for various favours. Becky, said Nancy, had told them she had married and was now called Mrs Sullivan and that she was looking for a servant girl. Nancy produced the letter Rebecca had written from Hope Cottage near Winchester, which was signed "Mrs Sullivan" but said she had heard nothing more, and she did not know where Eliza was. Nancy and her husband Bash were "evidently greatly troubled that such a stigma as that of decoying a girl away should be attached to them."

This falling out between Mrs Armstrong and Nancy had all come about because of the *Pall Mall Gazette* story about the girl bought for £5. Such a furore had been caused by the Maiden Tribute articles that the paper had been read in impoverished districts of London where a large number of adults were illiterate and such high-brow publications, even at a penny a copy, were beyond their means as well as their cultural horizon. However, Mrs Armstrong could read and so could some of the neighbours. Many of the little 'scholars' in the street, as schoolchildren were known, could read as well. When they came to the story in the Monday edition of the *Gazette* which told of the "child of thirteen bought for £5" rumours began to circulate. Mrs Armstrong, learning of these rumours, had got hold of the newspaper and read it herself. She had then accused her neighbour Nancy of fooling her into letting Eliza go with her friend from Claridge's.

The bits of evidence were circumstantial, and there was always hope that any day a letter would arrive from Eliza saying where she was and how she was getting on. But her silence was worrying. The simplest way of discovering whether or not Eliza was the girl the *Gazette* had written about would have been to get in touch with the newspaper editor himself. But this did not occur to

Mrs Armstrong who clearly could not imagine that anyone on the newspaper was responsible for the decoying of her daughter. This impression was perhaps heightened by the fact that the *Gazette*, on the evening of Monday 13 July, published an abbreviated version of the *Lloyd's Weekly* report on the proceedings at Marylebone Magistrates Court. Headlined "A Missing Daughter" it included this extract:

> "Witness said her girl was only thirteen years of age, and after having read what had recently been published in an evening newspaper she greatly feared some harm had overtaken her daughter."

There was no mention of the mother shedding tears. It was a very odd story for the *Gazette* to print appearing as it did on a page covering unrest in Ireland, a shooting in Kent, a balloon contest at Alexandra Palace and a court report on the alleged rape of a thirteen-year-old maid by her master. Was the intention to put a distance between the £5 virgin story of 6 July and this mother's search for her daughter?

"Nothing to do with us!" it seemed to imply.

Whether or not Mrs Armstrong saw the item in the *Gazette* we do not know. It is unlikely, but the *Lloyd's Weekly* reporters would have taken note and perhaps guessed that the *Gazette* was trying to throw them off the scent. As far as Mrs Armstrong was concerned, she simply wanted her daughter back with a reassurance that she had not been "tampered with" like the girl Lily. But if Eliza was the girl the *Gazette* had called Lily then she had been sold to a brothel, and Mrs Armstrong herself was branded a drunken mother who did not care a damn.

The will to believe it was all a mistake, and that the similarities of the *Gazette* story and the circumstances of Eliza's disappearance were just a coincidence, must have been very strong. Lisson Grove might be a slum in some people's eyes, but it was not a place where little girls were sold by their mothers for any sum of money. Except, that is, in the vivid imagination of the *Gazette*'s editor, W. T. Stead. What then, was Charles Street really like, and was it a place where a mother might be expected to put her daughter 'on the market'?

Chapter Three
A Victorian slum

If the huddle of streets just to the west of Regents Park had not been razed to the ground to make way for improved dwellings for the working classes just before the turn of the century, the hovels of Charles Street, Lisson Grove might in time have become bijou town houses for the gentrifying middle classes. 'Charming Victorian home with period features' the Estate Agents would coo. 'Just a short stroll from the green spaces of Regents Park and the shops of Marylebone High Street.'

Charles Street in the parish of Marylebone was an enclave of desperate poverty in a veritable sea of wealth. When the chimney sweep Charles Armstrong set up home there in the 1870s behind the front doors of each of the little houses there was always more than one family.

Every ten years, the British government conducted a census of the national population, listing the occupants of each house and institution in the country. The 1881 enumerator's record for Charles Street, written out on official forms in copper-plate script, reveals an astonishing crush of humanity. At No. 32 are found the Armstrongs: Charles and his wife, Elizabeth, aged then 38 and 33, and their four children, Eliza aged thirteen, her younger sister, also Eliza aged nine, sons John and Robert aged seven and two. In the same house live Frank Woodward, a costermonger, aged 45, his wife Sarah, 42, two young girls who are 'boarders', aged ten and eight, and two women lodgers aged 40 and 61: a tailoress and an 'ironer'. That is twelve altogether, but there were still more people living at No. 32: a widow, Jane Gunningham, aged 60, and her three unmarried sons, a 26 year old carman, a 20 year old costermonger and a shop boy aged 18.

The Armstrongs lived in just one room, as did most of the families in Charles Street and in the neighbouring roads, which together formed this little slum district in

Lisson Grove. Like Charles Armstrong, the chimney sweep, most of the poor here were not idlers but provided services without which London's millions, and the wealthy in particular, could not have survived.

The carmen were the van drivers of the day, making deliveries all over the capital in their horse-drawn wagons: everything from fruit and vegetables to furniture. Costermongers were the mobile street sellers who also worked the markets in the poor districts. Laundresses were there to ensure that the shop-keepers and the carriage classes had clean sheets on their beds. Needlewomen and machinists made the fine clothes for the social round of the upper crust's 'Season' in the West End. These, and the fire-wood choppers and a host of other 'penny capitalists', did the donkey work of the richest city in the world.

But their livelihood was precarious: most work was seasonal, the chimney sweeps, for example, getting most custom with the first chill winds of early autumn when Londoners began to light their fires and found them choked with soot. In summer there was less work and money was short: wives would bring in a few shillings selling flowers or finding cleaning jobs, and the older girls could go as servants to nearby houses.

In the 1880s, the great repository of poverty in London was in the East End, the vast region of docklands, sweated trades and foul smelling industries. But there were enclaves of it everywhere, even in the heart of the West End. The true extent of hardship in the midst of riches was unknown. Poverty was a burning social concern for the politicians and philanthropists of the capital. For some it was simply a disgrace, for others a sewer from which flowed a tide of immorality, and for some a simmering threat to social stability. Impoverished, filthy, criminal London was often likened to a 'savage' country which could only been brought back to civilisation by the kind of missionary work that the churches had taken to the farthest outposts of the Empire.

Slums like Charles Street, Lisson Grove, while ignored by the mass of the respectable population, were not left entirely alone. In the early 1880s there appeared on the streets an apparition which was greeted with a mixture of anger and disdain. Men and women dressed in a mock-military uniform, all buttons and bonnets, blowing brass instruments and rattling tambourines marched into Lisson Grove and set up a hall in which unfamiliar hymns were sung to the tunes of Music Hall favourites such as *Champagne Charlie*. At their meetings and on street corners, the locals were astounded to see women preachers. On Saturday nights, when they were drowning their sorrows in the Marquis of Anglesey pub, known locally as 'The Black Man' from its popularity with chimney sweeps, these 'Hallelujah Lassies' would go amongst them trying to sell a little paper called *War Cry*. The intrusion was never welcomed—quite a few of the regulars could not read anyway—and the bold young bonneted women could be roughly treated. In its first decades, the Salvation Army suffered a great deal of physical violence, and their experience in Lisson Grove was no exception.

It was not just the poor who found the Sally Army unsettling. The Established churches, who wrung their hands with anguish at the un-Godliness of the slum-dwellers, regarded the Army as vulgar, and many a man of the cloth lost a daughter to them. It was regarded by clergymen as a kind of cult which could spirit away young girls attracted by the novel status women could have and that they were denied in the churches. The Salvation Army, in its early days, was revolutionary and threatening, its founders, the massively bearded Methodist minister, William Booth, and Catherine, his strong-willed wife, almost demonic public figures.

In the slums and the poor districts of London, the Salvation Army sought to raise up the fallen through conversion to their brand Christianity. They preached against the demon drink and had a mission to rescue those whose lives were lived in sin. Bramwell Booth, the founder's son, who was given the title Chief of Staff in the mid-1880s, became involved with his wife in the great swathe of moral purity movements, one aim of which was to provide refuges for prostitutes who wanted to abandon their humiliating, and often dangerous, trade. Fallen women, who had been led into vice by cruel masters were the Mary Magdalenes of Victorian society, and their resurrection had a special poignancy for philanthropic women from the upper classes.

From time to time those who wished to shake the comfortable classes out of their apathy would publish shocking revelations about the conditions in which the poor lived. Well-meaning though these pamphleteers were, they had a tendency to tar all the under-classes of the capital with the same black brush. Anyone eking out a living as a chimney sweep or a dustman, a laundress or a needle worker, was likely to be branded a drunk and lacking in any kind of sexual morality. One such pamphlet, published anonymously in 1883 and given wide circulation was entitled 'The Bitter Cry of Outcast London'. The author, or authors, had descended to the depths and came back with a horrifying report of vice, misery and squalor, of families in a single room, of barefoot children and drunken parents. Here is an extract:

"Who can wonder that young girls wander off into a life of immorality, which promises release from such conditions? Who can wonder that the public-house is 'the Elysian field' of the tired toiler? IMMORALITY is but the natural outcome of conditions like these. 'Marriage', it had been said, 'as an institution, is not fashionable in these districts'. And this is only the bare truth. Ask if the men and women living together in these rookeries are married, and your simplicity will cause a smile. Nobody knows. Nobody cares. Nobody expects that they are. In exceptional cases only could your question be answered in the affirmative. Incest is common; and no form of vice and sensuality causes surprise or attracts attention."

This ghastly vision of London's poor, of places like Charles Street, was given widespread coverage by Stead in the the *Pall Mall Gazette*. It shocked Parliament into setting up a Royal Commission on working-class housing, and was a triumph for Stead's campaigning journalism. The mystery of the pamphlet's author has never been entirely solved, but it was believed to be a Congregationalist minister, Andrew Mearns, who was assisted in his research by two other men. Whatever its real merits as a piece of social investigation, its picture of depravity was not questioned by the *Pall Mall Gazette*.

There were at this time, however, investigations which took more trouble to understand the lifestyles of the poor. One was by the Social Democratic Federation which estimated that a quarter of London's population lived below the breadline. The author of this piece, Henry Hyndman, was in a circle of social reformers which included the fabulously wealthy ship-owner, Charles Booth. Charles and his elder brother, Andrew, had made their fortune in the rubber trade between Brazil and Liverpool. After a bout of ill-health, Charles moved to London where he became involved in the organisation of relief funds for the poor. And he argued with Hyndman about the extent of poverty in London: he did not believe it could not be as high as 25 per cent of the population.

Booth decided to make his own study of the London poor, beginning in 1884. It took him twenty years to complete and he paid for it all out of his own pocket, the equivalent of several million pounds at today's prices.

On occasion he took lodging in the East End of London, living anonymously with poor families, but most of the survey work was carried out by the capital's ubiquitous School Board visitors. The introduction of compulsory State education for children aged five to thirteen divided the whole of England and Wales into school districts, and the 'Board Men' were appointed to ensure all children attended. Booth engaged these unpopular local officers to make notes on every single street in London and, with the addition of remarks from local clergy and policemen, drew a social class picture of the entire capital. The detailed work grew into six volumes of text, and Booth used the basic material to draw maps of every district. These survive today as the most remarkable visual representation ever made of the social class jigsaw of a great city.

A colour code was devised to categorise the status of every street:

> BLACK: Lowest class. Vicious, semi-criminal.
> DARK BLUE: Very poor, casual. Chronic want.
> LIGHT BLUE: Poor. 18s. to 21s. a week for a moderate family.
> PURPLE: Mixed. Some comfortable others poor.
> PINK: Fairly comfortable. Good ordinary earnings.
> RED: Middle class. Well-to-do.
> YELLOW: Upper-middle and Upper classes. Wealthy.

In the first volume of his *Life and Labour of the People in London* published in 1891 Booth said of Lisson Grove, the district where the Armstrongs lived:

> "That there should be 50,000 people, half of whom are poor, living together in the midst of wealthy West London, is remarkable, and I know of no sufficient explanation (A footnote suggests that some of the poor had moved to Lisson Grove when their homes were knocked down for the building of New Oxford Street). Of this population, the poor half are

said to be friendly but very ignorant. Savage rather than bad. The men mostly casual labourers and hawkers, while the women do washing and charring. Below these there is a sub-stratum of thieves, cadgers, common prostitutes, and other loose and loafing men and women. Throughout, drink is very prevalent. The people and the place have a character of their own; different from East London, very different from Central London; rather more like some parts south of the Thames; but with a difference due probably to the peculiarity of the West End situation, surrounded by the houses of the rich."

The social class map of the area illustrates his point. Coloured yellow were Dorset Square, home to the Grossmith brothers who wrote the satire *Diary of a Nobody* about the aspiring Victorian clerk Mr Pooter, and Blandford Square where the novelist Georg Eliot had lived in the 1860s. There were streets of brick-red respectability where the comfortably off trades people lived, many of them above their shops, and streets of dark blue where the investigators had judged the residents to be near or below the poverty line. There were a few patches of black which Booth's investigators had identified as the enclaves of the "vicious and semi-criminal classes". Charles Street, Lisson Grove was not one of them. It, and the roads running parallel of Great James Street, were all dark blue—impoverished but largely "honest".

Booth reckoned that only about two per cent of London's poor were of the lowest, criminal or semi-criminal class. A far larger number of the poor attempted to live as respectable a life as possible in circumstances that were almost impossibly difficult. When he took lodgings in the East End, Booth encountered drunken mothers and violent fathers, but for the most part he was impressed by the sense of social responsibility most families had. For his written account of the poorest classes he had an extra division identifying five layers of deprivation from A, the very lowest, to B, not much higher, and C, D and E with rising levels of income and comfort. Those he lodged with and befriended were in classes C and above and he had this to say of the families:

> "The children in class E, and still more in class D, have when young less chance of surviving than those of the rich, but I certainly think their lives are happier, free from the paraphernalia of servants, nurses and governesses, always provided they have decent parents. They are more likely to suffer from spoiling than from harshness, for they are made much of, being commonly the pride of their mother, who will sacrifice much to see them prettily dressed, and the delight of their father's heart. This makes the home, and the happiness of the parents; but it is not this, it is the constant occupation, which makes the children's lives so happy. They have their regular school hours, and when at home, as soon as they are old enough, there is 'mother' to help, and they have their numbers of little friends.
>
> In class E they have for a playground the back yard, in class D the even greater delights of the street. With really bad parents the story may be different, but men and women may be very bad and yet love their children and make them happy. In the summer holidays, when my carman [ie in the same lodging] had a load to carry for some building in the country he would take two of the children with him. Supplied with bread and butter and 2d to buy fruit, they would start off early and come home in the evening, happy, tired and dirty, to tell of all the sights they had seen."

In what category Booth would have put the Armstrong's of Charles Street, it is not possible to say. But his touching description of childhood in poor districts is close to

Eliza's experience up to the first sweltering days of June: she went to Board School, she helped care for her baby brother and around the house, she had been on trips out of London and she loved her mother and father. Though her parents would be judged a rough pair by more respectable classes, the mother drinking too much and given to swearing, the father occasionally violent, in their own class and on their own terms they were certainly doing right by their children.

Chapter Four
"A child of thirteen bought for £5"

The story of the £5 virgin, as written in the 6th July edition of the *Gazette*, is worth giving in full. It incorporates many of the elements of the trade in virgins which the Maiden Tribute investigation claimed to have uncovered elsewhere. In fact it pretty much followed a script devised by Stead in which all the elements of his wider investigation in to the procuring of virgins were covered: the reformed brothel keeper, the midwife who examined the girls to make sure they were 'pure', the drugging of the victim and so on. 'Lily' was said to have been bought from a brothel which, in Stead's mind, was a kind of 'shop' where mothers vied with each other to get their daughters sold for a bounty.

As a manifesto to persuade Parliament that the age of thirteen was far too young for girls to be accounted responsible for their own seduction it was more or less perfect. 'Lily' was just the right age, she was entirely innocent herself and she was duped into going off with a stranger. It added poignancy to the story that she was not an orphan or the child of a prostitute already in the trade. This, then, is the story Stead wrote, along with some annotations which Mrs Armstrong and her neighbours might have made as they read it, suggesting that Lily might well have been little Eliza Armstrong.

> "At the beginning of this Derby week, a woman, an old hand in the work of procuration, entered a brothel in ——— st. M———, kept by an old acquaintance, and opened negotiations for the purchase of a maid. One of the women who lodged in the house had a sister as yet untouched. Her mother was far away, her father was dead. The child was living in the house, and in all probability would be seduced and follow the profession of her elder sister."

(Eliza went away with "Mrs Sullivan" on Derby Day, 3rd June, the M could stand for Marylebone, but there were no brothels in Charles Street.)

"The child was between thirteen and fourteen, and after some bargaining it was agreed that she should be handed over to the procuress for the sum of £5. The maid was wanted, it was said, to start a house with, and there was no disguise on either side that the sale was to be effected for immoral purposes. While the negotiations were going on, a drunken neighbour came into the house, and so little concealment was then used, that she speedily became aware of the nature of the transaction. So far from being horrified at the proposed sale of the girl, she whispered eagerly to the seller, 'Don't you think she would take our Lily? I think she would suit.' Lily was her own daughter, a bright, fresh-looking little girl, who was thirteen years old last Christmas. The bargain, however, was made for the other child, and Lily's mother felt she had lost her market."

(It is difficult to know what to make of this. Where did the information come from? Is this about Eliza whose birthday was not at Christmas but in April. Maybe it was not Eliza after all.)

"The next day, Derby Day as it happened, was fixed for the delivery of this human chattel. But as luck would have it, another sister of the child who was to be made over to the procuress heard of the proposed sale. She was living respectably in a situation, and on hearing of the fate reserved for the little one she lost no time in persuading her dissolute sister to break off the bargain. When the woman came for her prey the bird had flown. Then came the chance of Lily's mother. The brothel-keeper sent for her, and offered her a sovereign for her daughter. The woman was poor, dissolute, and indifferent to everything but drink.

The father, who was also a drunken man, was told his daughter was going to a situation. He received the news with indifference, without even inquiring where she was going to."

(Again, the reference to Derby Day. Mrs Armstrong did drink and had sometimes been fined for being drunk and disorderly. Charles Armstrong, her husband, was not a drunk, but did believe his daughter had gone to be a servant.)

"The brothel-keeper having thus secured possession of the child, then sold her to the procuress in place of the child whose sister had rescued her from her destined doom for £5—£3 paid down and the remaining £2 after her virginity had been professionally certified. The little girl, all unsuspecting the purpose for which she was destined, was told that she must go with this strange woman to a situation. The procuress, who was well up to her work, took her away, washed her, dressed her up neatly, and sent her to bid her parents good-bye. The mother was so drunk she hardly recognised her daughter. The father was hardly less indifferent. The child left her home, and was taken to the woman's lodging in A——street."

(When Mrs Armstrong had agreed for Eliza to go with Mrs Sullivan, new clothes had been bought for the girl. A——street could have been Albany Street on the other side of Regent's Park.)

"The first step had thus been taken. But it was necessary to procure the certification of her virginity —a somewhat difficult task, as the child was absolutely ignorant of the nature of the transaction which had transferred her from home to the keeping of this strange, but apparently kind-hearted woman. Lily was a little cockney child, one of those who, by the thousand, annually develop into the servants of the poorer middle-class. She had been at school, could read and write, and although her spelling was extraordinary, she was able to express herself with much force and decision. Her experience of the world was limited to the London quarter in which she had been born. With the exception of two school trips to Richmond and one to Epping Forest, she had never been in the country in her life, nor had she ever even seen the Thames excepting at Richmond."

(Richmond and Epping Forest were the only two places Eliza had been away from Charles Street. It was not an outing organised by a brothel: she had gone with the Sunday school.)

"She was an industrious, warm-hearted little thing, a hardy English child, slightly coarse in texture, with dark black eyes, and short, sturdy figure. Her education was slight. She spelled write "right," for instance, and her grammar was very shaky. But she was a loving, affectionate child, whose kindly feeling for the drunken mother who sold her into nameless infamy was very touching to behold. In a little letter of hers which I once saw, plentifully garlanded with kisses, there was the following ill-spelled childish verse:—

As I was in bed
Some little forths (thoughts) gave (came) in my head.
I forth (thought) of one, I forth (thought) of two;
But first of all I forth (thought) of you.

The poor child was full of delight at going to her new situation, and clung affectionately to the keeper who was taking her away—where, she knew not."

(Eliza was fond of her mother, she could read and write, she was a helpful girl described by her mother as "a good little scrubber." How the *Gazette* had got hold of a verse she had written was a mystery. Mrs Armstrong had had no letters from Eliza.)

"The first thing to be done after the child was fairly severed from home was to secure the certificate of virginity without which the rest of the purchase-money would not be forthcoming. In order to avoid trouble she was taken in a cab to the house of a midwife, whose skill in pronouncing upon the physical evidences of virginity is generally recognised in the profession. The examination was very brief and completely satisfactory. But the youth, the complete innocence of the girl, extorted pity even from the hardened heart of the old abortionist. 'The poor little thing,' she exclaimed. 'She is so small, her pain will be extreme. I hope you will not be too cruel with her'—as if to lust when fully roused the very acme of agony on the part of the victim has not a fierce delight."

(If Lily was Eliza then she had been indecently assaulted. Why had the Secret Commission not prevented this from happening?).

"To quiet the old lady, the agent of the purchaser asked if she could supply anything to dull the pain. She produced a small phial of chloroform. 'This,' she said, 'is the best. My clients find this much the most effective.' The keeper took the bottle, but unaccustomed to anything but drugging by the administration of sleeping potions, she would infallibly have poisoned the child had she not discovered by experiment that the liquid burned the mouth when an attempt was made to swallow it. £1 1s. was paid for the certificate of virginity—which was verbal and not written—while £1 10s. more was charged for the chloroform, the net value of which was probably less than a shilling. An arrangement was made that if the child was badly injured Madame would patch it up to the best of her ability, and then the party left the house."

(Who made the arrangement? Why was this allowed to happen?)

"From the midwife's the innocent girl was taken to a house of ill fame, No. —, P———— street, Regent-street, where, notwithstanding her extreme youth, she was admitted without question. She was taken up stairs, undressed, and put to bed, the woman who bought her putting her to sleep. She was rather restless, but under the influence of chloroform she soon went over. Then the woman withdrew. All was quiet and still. A few moments later the door opened, and the purchaser entered the bedroom. He closed and locked the door. There was a brief silence. And then there rose a wild and piteous cry—not a loud shriek, but a helpless, startled scream like the bleat of a frightened lamb. And the child's voice was heard crying, in accents of terror, 'There's a man in the room! Take me home; oh, take me home!' And then all once more was still."

(Could poor Eliza have suffered this?)

"That was but one case among many, and by no means the worst. It only differs from the rest because I have been able to verify the facts. Many a similar cry will be raised this very night in the brothels of London, unheeded by man, but not unheard by the pitying ear of Heaven—

For the child's sob in the darkness curseth deeper
Than the strong man in his wrath."

The series of clues in the Lily story that suggested she might be Eliza were not the only reason Mrs Armstrong had to fear that her daughter had been sold to a brothel. It seems likely that her attention had first been drawn to the Maiden Tribute story by a kindly middle-aged gentleman called Mr Edward Thomas. He kept a refuge for fallen women in the nearby Marylebone Road and had followed the Maiden Tribute story as well as the sequel in *Lloyd's Weekly*. He probably provided *Lloyd's Weekly* with the tip-off in the first place.

The name of Nancy Broughton's friend, Rebecca Jarrett (spelled Jerrett in *Lloyd's*), who had taken Eliza Armstrong from Charles Street, filled him with foreboding, for he knew Jarrett as a prostitute and keeper of 'gay' houses. She might, or might not be, reformed, but it seemed to him that she was the woman in the Maiden Tribute story of the child thirteen bought for five pounds. It was Mr Thomas's view that Mrs Armstrong, rough-tongued as she was and liable to drinking bouts, was otherwise a good, honest mother and that it was inconceivable that she had sold her daughter. He befriended her, and gave her money to help her find Eliza.

While Mr Thomas and *Lloyd's Weekly* continued their search for Eliza, believing her to be the 'Lily' of The Maiden Tribute story, the police, instructed by the Marylebone Magistrates, treated Mrs Armstrong's daughter simply as a missing person. They had no special interest in whether or not Eliza was the girl described by the *Pall Mall Gazette*. A visit to Charles Street would be sufficient to provide an officer with the evidence required to further his enquiries.

Chapter Five
The mystery of Hope Cottage

On 14 July, just three days after the visit from the *Lloyd's Weekly* reporter, Nancy Broughton opened her door in Charles Street to a soulful looking gentleman who announced himself as Inspector Edward Borner of Scotland Yard. He had been called in to help with the hunt for Eliza and had been to see Mrs Armstrong. He wanted to see the letter Mrs Broughton had received from her friend Becky Jarrett saying she had Eliza with her. She had received it on 10 June, a week after Eliza left Charles Street with Becky, now calling herself Mrs Sullivan. It read:

> "Dear Nancy, I dare say you are looking for this letter from me, but I am so happy to tell you that Eliza is all right and doing well with me. I have bought her a lot more clothes. She looks quite happy. She sends her love to her mother and father and to you. I am on a visit, and she is with me stopping for a week, but we go home next week. My love to all and Jack (Nancy's husband), and her mother and father and to all at your home. I shall soon come and see you again, if you will let me. My love to all—From yours truly Rebecca, Mrs Sullivan."

The address given was Hope Cottage, High Cliff, Winchester.

The next day Inspector Borner went down to Winchester and found Hope Cottage. It was closed up and he had no way of getting in. He then went to see Mrs Josephine Butler, a close friend of the *Pall Mall Gazette*'s editor, W. T. Stead.

Mrs Butler was well known as a campaigner for women's rights and social reform who had established the Hope Cottage refuge for 'fallen women' and lived nearby. Her husband was Canon of Winchester Cathedral. Mrs

Butler refused to tell Inspector Borner anything. She did not like policemen, she explained later, and had a rule that she would have little or nothing to do with them. In any case, she had been sworn to secrecy by the Chief Director of the Secret Commission. However, she let slip that Rebecca Jarrett was connected with the Salvation Army.

The following day, Inspector Borner went to the headquarters of the Salvation Army at 101 Queen Victoria Street and asked to see Mr Bramwell Booth, Chief of Staff. His notes on this meeting read:

> "I am Inspector Borner; I have come to see you with respect to a case that appeared in *Lloyd's Newspaper* of last Sunday about a girl named Eliza Armstrong; I have been referred to you by Mrs Josephine Butler of Winchester"—He (Booth) said: "Yes, I know something of the case, but I cannot tell you exactly where the child is at present, but if you like I will have inquiries made during the day, and let you know".

Mr Booth said he would send the address on to Mr Munroe, Commissioner of Police at Scotland Yard, if he was able to find it.

There the matter rested, for a while. Inspector Borner did not think it necessary to question Stead at the office of the *Gazette* in Northampton Street as he was confident Mr Booth would tell him where he could find Eliza. At this stage in his inquiry there was no intention of prosecuting anybody: his task was simply to return the girl to her mother. He was not really concerned about whether Eliza was 'Lily'—his task was simply to find her, and he was well on his way as Bramwell Booth would clearly point him in the right direction. Inspector Borner then took his annual leave travelling to the Fenland town of Wisbech where he could be contacted by telegraph, if necessary.

Meanwhile, *Lloyd's Weekly* had continued with its own inquiries. Some time after Inspector Borner had been down to Hope Cottage, a reporter took Mrs Armstrong herself, believing Eliza must be somewhere nearby. The account of this day at Winchester published by *Lloyd's Weekly Newspaper* was not encouraging. It read:

"On arriving at High Cliff the house was found shut up. It was a two-storey cottage of six rooms. In reply to questions the neighbours stated that it was generally known as 'The farm for fallen women' and that it was a place which had been used by some of the Salvation Army people to keep fallen women and girls, owing, however, to the exposure which had been made in *Lloyd's* newspaper a month ago, and which the people said had come like a thunderbolt into the place, some of the people connected with it had gone away.

Speaking of the character of the place, it was generally assented that it had been a nuisance to the neighbourhood, and that the people inside and outside connected with it 'Were a rummy lot'. Asked why, they replied: 'Because they fetched bad women, and nice girls from where they could get them, and shut them up for together for days and nights unattended without any supervision, or any one to mind them. Owing to the noise and want of control the place and people in it became so objectionable that they would have to appeal to the sanitary authorities.'

The reporter was told that, left to their own devices, the inmates of Hope Cottage quarrelled and fought, but the noise was even worse when the Salvation Army captain came to drill them and filled the night with 'Hallelujah choruses'. When the matron of Hope Cottage, known as the Magdalene Home, had gone away it was said she was on 'an important mission.' They did not know what this was until they read stories about Eliza Armstrong being taken away by a stout woman who walked lame and was known as Rebecca Jarrett.

All the furniture had now gone from Hope Cottage, taken away by a Pickford's van the previous week and had been sent to a place called 'The Home of Rest Cannon Street' in Winchester." (This was set up by Josephine Butler for terminally ill prostitutes, or 'dying Magdalenes' as she called them.)

The reporter followed with Mrs Armstrong and they were ushered in by "an elderly, ladylike person" who said, without being asked:

> "I know what you have come for, and why you have gained admittance this way. You have come thinking to see that lost girl from London here…"

This matron, a Mrs Hillier sympathised with Mrs Armstrong over the loss of Eliza and said that it was unfortunate what had happened. The reporter appealed to her to tell them what she knew she of the matter.

> "She exonerated Mrs. Josephine Butler from any blame in the transactions. She said that when they found out that Rebecca Jerrett (*sic*) had been away from her duties as the matron of the refuge she was greatly surprised. She wrote to Mrs. Bramwell Booth upon the matter, but received from her a reply stating that they must not blame poor Becky for that as she had been engaged in other business in connection with the work in London."

Mrs Armstrong and the reporter were told that Rebecca Jarrett had been very ill and close to death when she vowed to change her ways and asked Mrs Bramwell Booth and Mrs Butler to save her. The matron told them:

> "She confessed that she had for a long time been a brothel keeper, and one of the worst procuresses of London. She told us of crimes almost incredible; and as we prayed for her life she made a vow that if God would only restore her she would lead a reformed life, and devote herself to rescue work."

The reporter then came to the point of their visit to Winchester:

> "I will not ask you any questions as to the purpose for which this child Armstrong was got away but we have arrived at this fact: that she was decoyed from her parents by a professedly religious woman, and that woman the acknowledged matron of the Winchester home."
>
> Answer: "Yes"
>
> "Do you think that act, or that anybody of religionists have the right to decoy a child from its mother?"
>
> Answer: "No."
>
> "Do you consider it a religious act when that child is inquired for by its parents, for them to hide the child whereabouts and give false addresses?"
>
> Answer: "No"
>
> "Do you consider it a either a religious or justifiable act for Mr. Bramwell Booth or anyone else, when he knows that this poor woman is hunting everywhere for her lost child, to cause her to run from place to place, and at last get the child out of the country?"
>
> Answer: "No, and I think the mother is perfectly justified in doing all she can to get her child back. I know I should."

The reporter left it at that, satisfied that Eliza was not being hidden in a refuge in Winchester. He and Mrs Armstrong then went to Canon Butler's house where a servant assured them there were no girls being kept there. So the two of them returned to London with a better idea of who Rebecca Jarrett was and how she had come to be associated with the Salvation Army, but no wiser about Eliza's whereabouts.

55

Chapter Six
The Mansion House Committee

While *Lloyd's Weekly* and Mrs Armstrong were in Winchester in search of Eliza, the first of a bizarre series of meetings was taking place in the City of London. Though Stead was from a Congregationalist background, he became a close friend of Cardinal Henry Manning, the Catholic convert from a distinguished political family. Stead also wrote regularly to Edward White Benson who had been enthroned as Archbishop of Canterbury in 1883 and had discussed the Maiden Tribute campaign with him. Because he did not name anyone in his expose of vice in the capital, and concerned that he might be accused of reporting mere hearsay, Stead called together a 'committee' of the great and the good whose integrity was unimpeachable. The members would be shown his confidential research material in private. This committee would not be able to divulge anything new but would simply vouch publicly for authenticity of Stead's Maiden Tribute claims.

With the aid of the seventy-five-year-old Benjamin Scott, Chamberlain of the City of London, Stead was able to assemble on four occasions at the Mansion House, Cardinal Manning, Archbishop Benson, John Morely a Member of Parliament, and John Reid a barrister and Queens Counsel. No official record of these proceedings seems to have been kept: it was an ad hoc gathering with no legal or formal powers, more a kind of self-inflicted show trial for Stead and his so-called Secret Commission, which was becoming less secret by the day.

The sittings of the so-called "Mansion House Committee" or commission, took place on four days in July, the first on 15th. Stead appeared intermittently, it seems. He had imagined that he was in control of witnesses that would appear, but he was wrong. At one hearing, Mr Edward Thomas, the man who kept a refuge in the Marylebone Road and had taken up Mrs Armstrong's cause, turned up, and brought Mrs Armstrong with him. She made a moving appeal for the return of her daughter Eliza who she believed must be the same girl as the Lily in the Maiden Tribute articles. Stead was there, and watched her wringing her hands, but remained silent and unmoved. In fact he left the committee hearing as she was making her appeal.

When the Mansion House Committee sat, Inspector Borner was on holiday, so he missed his chance to interview Rebecca Jarrett who made an appearance on 19th July. In any case, he had an agreement with Bramwell Booth of the Salvation Army that the address where Eliza could be found would be forwarded to his chief while he was away. By the time he was back at Scotland Yard the girl should have been found and reunited with her parents. But on his return from holiday, Inspector Borner discovered that no address had been handed in at Scotland Yard. On 31 July, by which time Eliza had been missing for nearly two months, Borner went back to see Booth at the Salvation Army headquarters in Queen Victoria Street. He made notes on the conversation, jotting down Booth's response:

> "Since I saw you last my position as regards the girl Armstrong is very much altered; she is now under my control, and in service with a lady on the Continent; she is being well brought up and educated as a Christian."

To this the Inspector replied:

> "I have come from Mr Cooke, the Magistrate of Marylebone Police Court." Whereupon Mr Booth responded: "We shall be prepared to make application that the child should become a ward in Chancery rather than return to the same kind of living."

(Booth had clearly got the notion that Eliza had been working as a prostitute: in reality she did not have a "living" in Charles Street).

Mrs Armstrong had written a letter to Booth, signed both for herself and her husband Charles, but she had received no reply. Eliza's whereabouts were still not forthcoming. Inspector Borner asked Booth if he would agree for him to bring Mrs Armstrong to see him. Reluctantly Booth assented, but he told the Inspector that the woman was a drunkard and Charles Street a bad place.

After consultation with Mr Cooke, the Marylebone Magistrate, Borner went to see Mrs Armstrong. Accompanied by another Inspector, they went back to Queen Victoria Street. Bramwell Booth was very deaf and would conduct his conversations with a huge ear trumpet the size of gramophone horn. He sized up Mrs Armstrong, aimed his giant hearing aid and heard her out. Borner recorded the exchange:

Mrs Armstrong: "I have come to speak to you about my child, I want her back."

Mr Booth: "You cannot have her, for she is in the South of France with a lady, being well brought up and educated."

Mrs Armstrong: "Why cannot I have her back?"

Mr Booth: "Because I have been to great expense: have you £100?"

Mrs Armstrong: "No Sir, I am only a poor woman"

Mr Booth: "Well, that is about what it cost me; why don't you let her remain? I will pay you her wages monthly, or how you like, and I will give you her address, and you can communicate with her, and when she comes to England you can see her; if you will sign a receipt I will pay you the wages due to her."

At this Booth turned to Inspector Borner and enquired: "What do you think? Two or three shillings a week?"

Borner declined any involvement and said it was up to the parents.

Mrs Armstrong: "No, Sir, I want my child back."

Inspector Borner then said to Booth: "The mother seems to be under the impression that the child has been tampered with or outraged."

Mr Booth: "I can assure you that when the child was brought to me she was pure."

Borner noted: "... the mother clasped her hands together and said 'Thank God for that' then burst out crying."

Mr Booth continued his reassurance: "She was examined by a medical gentleman, and I have a certificate, and if Mr Cooke would like to see it I will find it."

Inspector Borner said he thought that would be unnecessary, though he would mention it to the magistrate.

There was a pause, then Booth continued: "Why don't you let her remain?" To which Mrs Armstrong retorted: "Because I want her back to take before a Magistrate to prove that I never sold her."

Booth replied: "She would not know whether she was sold."

Mrs Armstrong disagreed: "She would know whether she was sold. Oh yes, a girl of thirteen would know whether she was sold or not."

Then, according to the Inspector's report, Booth got up from his seat and went over to his desk. He said to Mrs Armstrong:

"Well, if you are determined to have her back there, this is the address, that is all I can do for you."

He handed over a piece of paper on which there was written out the name of Monsieur Theodore Berard in the town of Loriol-sur-Drome, France (midway between Lyon and Marseille). How it was that Eliza had landed up there was a mystery, but Mrs Armstrong wrote to her straight away.

Chapter Seven
Anger in Charles Street

By the first week in August the disappearance of Eliza Armstrong was a regular feature in *Lloyd's Weekly* and the local newspapers around Lisson Grove such as the *Marylebone Mercury*. Although only bits and pieces of the story involving the Salvation Army were known, the word on the street was that Mrs Armstrong's daughter had been the victim of a strange, evangelical abduction involving a notorious ex-brothel keeper. At the same time the moral purity campaigners, confident that the Criminal Law Amendment Bill would go through, continued to hold rallies around the country. Tensions began to rise in many poor districts where the activities of the Salvation Army were not welcomed, and in Lisson Grove the antagonism reached a crescendo.

The *Marylebone Mercury* ran the following letter under the heading: "Love's Labours Lost". It was signed simply "Eye-Witness":

"Sir, A few days ago a benevolent lady, resident in Marylebone, who takes much interest in the poor of Lisson Grove and neighbourhood, paid a visit to Charles Street to sympathise with Mrs Armstrong in the distressing circumstances in which she is placed by the abduction of her daughter. Mrs Armstrong, evidently mistaking the mission of the lady, ordered her, I was informed, out of the house, and then, when she got her into the street, raised a cry that the lady was one of the persons concerned in the disappearance of the child and was related to the infamous Mrs Jarrett. The lady protested her innocence of the entire transaction, and explained the reason for her visit; but without avail.

A crowd of men, women and children speedily gathered, and set upon the lady, pushing her about and ultimately knocking her down on the ground, to the great danger of her life. The lady appealed for help to a well-dressed man who was passing, and he got the police to her assistance. By this time the crowd had increased to several hundreds, and they were hooting and shouting like maniacs. The police, with great difficulty, got the lady into a shop, and barricaded the door. The mob gathered in front of the shop, and threatened to break in the door and the windows if the ' procuress', as they called the lady, was not delivered up to them. Additional police arriving on the scene, the mob was beaten back, and a cab having being procured, the lady was got into it and the cabman drove rapidly off, the crowd finding vent to their rage in a volley of howls and groans. The benevolent lady was evidently much shaken by the rough handling she was subjected to."

In Lisson Grove, and in all likelihood in many other poor districts of London, the villain of the Armstrong story was not now the mother accused of selling her daughter but the do-gooder who spirited away young girls for their own, mysterious, moral purposes. Charles Street was not the kind of place that was anxiously awaiting the passing of the Criminal Law Amendment Act. What they were concerned about was the whereabouts of little Eliza and news of her well being.

Despite the assurance that Bramwell Booth had given Mrs Armstrong that Eliza had not been drugged and raped, as Stead's account of what happened to 'Lily' had suggested, the dogged pursuit of the case by *Lloyd's Weekly* had turned up some new and worrying evidence. It began with a tip off from a cab driver and led to a farcical scene in which both Mr and Mrs Armstrong and the *Lloyd's* reporter found themselves in a very strange establishment not far from Charles Street.

The eyes and ears of London after dark were the cab drivers. There were, at that time, more than 11,000 horse drawn cabs in London, over 7,000 "hansoms", two wheelers, and around 4,000 "broughams" which were four wheelers. Though they were all were registered with the police, London's 15,000 cabmen were regarded as a fairly rough bunch: every year about 2,000 of them were hauled before the magistrates for drunkenness, cruelty to their horses, wilful misbehaviour, loitering, obstruction and stopping on the wrong side of the road. The night-time cabbies were thought of as the roughest of all. Their fares would often be prostitutes and their clients and only a very unusual incident would be worth remarking on.

It was such a circumstance that prompted a cab driver to contact *Lloyd's Weekly*. He told them he had been called off his cab stand near Milton Street, off Dorset Square, close to Lisson Grove, at about 9.30 pm on Derby Night (the day Eliza had disappeared with Nancy's friend Becky) by two men and told to wait not outside a particular house, but just a short way from it:

> "When I stopped I saw a young girl about 13 or 14 come out of the gate. I thought she looked rather down. She was dressed in a dark, purple coloured frock, which was made long, and came down nearly to her boot tops. She also had on new sidesprung boots. I also noticed that she had a reddish straw hat, with a kind of yellow feather in the front. She did not appear to be crying, but she appeared as if she hardly knew what she was up to, nor where she was going, but that she had to wait for orders."

The cabman had told his wife about this strange fare he had had on Derby night, and they had considered going to the police because he thought there was some "foul play" going on. Then he had read about the missing girl and wondered if it was her. The cabman's story led to *Lloyd's*

Weekly reporter to the house in Milton Street where these odd goings on had taken place. This was his story:

"I (the un-named *Lloyd's* reporter) determined to take the mother there, and as a measure of precaution, resolved to have the father near at hand. I had heard that it might be rather difficult for me to get see the Madame, so I sent the mother forward and when she obtained admission I followed. An English servant said I could not see Madame without an introduction, but on my saying I would introduce myself, she ran back up some stairs, and we followed into what appeared to be a consulting room. The servant then ran out of another door through the yard into what looked like a glass house which seemed to have a bed in the centre with curtains round. The servant was heard exclaiming: 'There's a man in the house! There's a man in the house; and he's down in the room.'

A Frenchman appeared in a state of great excitement, and was followed by a second female. While they were talking and gesticulating violently, a large dog of the Newfoundland type was panting, barking, and tugging at his chain through the consulting door window, which was wide open. I told the Frenchman that I only wanted quietly to ask Madame a few questions, and when she had answered them we should both go away.

The parties went out eventually, Madame came. It was some minutes before we could get sufficient calmness to put a single question, and at first all knowledge of any girl was denied. Madame was then asked:

'Don't you remember a woman bringing a little girl here on Derby Day night?'

She hesitated, then shook her head, and said, 'Do you mean a good many weeks ago?'

'Yes; some weeks ago.'

'Do you mean a nice little girl that was brought by a big woman?', she said.

'Yes, that is the girl', I said

'She came with a big woman this high (putting her hand above her head to show her height)

'Yes.'

'And the woman walked lame with a stick?'

'Yes.'

'And it had a round knob on it? she said 'Oh, yes; why she put that stick on this table', 'Well, this person is that little girl's mother; and we want to know what you know about her?'

'I know nothing about her; I only did my business, and that is all I know about her' she said.

'Well, what was she brought here for?'

'For me to examine her.'

'And did you examine the girl?'

'Yes; she was not in the house long.'

'But why was she examined?'

'A gentleman wished it.' Turning to the mother she said, 'Yours was a beautiful little child.'

She was quite right, the mother said 'I know that'.

I then said: 'But what right had the woman to bring her for such a purpose?'

'I don't know. She said that she was her aunt that the girl belonged to her.'

'Who was the man?'

'I don't know I never saw him before.'

On certain other questions being asked, a fresh scene of excitement ensued, and one of the servants raised the cry of: 'Police!'

Mrs. Armstrong, fearing that I was going to be attacked, or that the dog might get loose, rushed out of the room, up the stairs, and along the passage calling to her husband: 'Charley, Charley; come in and fetch the police!'

Opening the door she let in her husband. Being a tall powerful man and a sweep in his working clothes, his demon like appearance had an electrical effect. The female servants ran back, the Frenchman seemed paralysed, and the old lady threw up her hands, while her eyes remained fixed on the figure before her. Mr. Armstrong was the first to break the silence by coolly saying

'Well you are a fine colour, all of you. Why you are all as white as turnips. What is the matter?'

His wife told him, and added something about liking to have her revenge on somebody. Upon hearing this I interposed, and we all quickly and quietly left the house."

Little by little, the diligent *Lloyd's Weekly* reporters were piecing the together the Lily story from the *Pall Mall Gazette*. There could be little doubt now that Lily and Eliza were one and the same girl. But Eliza had not yet been released by her captors, who appeared to be the Salvation Army, and until she was it would not be possible to say if everything that happened to Lily in the Maiden Tribute had, in reality, happened to Eliza. Though Mrs Armstrong was now in contact with senior police officers no action had been taken to force Bramwell Booth to hand her over. And nobody approached Stead himself.

Of Mrs Armstrong, the *Marylebone Mercury* wrote:

"What with the unsatisfactory result of the inquiries yet made after the missing girl, and the constant importunities of inquisitive strangers, the poor woman is completely prostrated. In the neighbourhood of Lisson Grove considerable surprise has been expressed at the strange revelations which have appeared in the public press, and many have been the expressions of sympathy conveyed to Mrs Armstrong in her great trouble. The Salvation Army, who recently opened a large establishment in the neighbourhood of Charles Street, are much blamed for the part they have played in the transaction, and a strong feeling prevails in the district that some explanation from members of the Booth family should be forthcoming."

By mid-August there had still been no word that Eliza was coming home. Stead must have been sharply aware at every stage of the unravelling of the mystery of the missing girl that he could have put everyone's mind at rest and simply owned up to what he had done. But he chose not to. Perhaps he still hoped it would all blow over and that Mrs Armstrong would give up. He was to say many times over the next few weeks and months that he did not really believe she wanted her daughter back. All her agitation was an attempt to convince people she did not sell her daughter. Although he was not privy to whatever was said in Charles Street on Derby Day, Stead had convinced himself that Rebecca Jarrett had told him the truth when she said she had bought Eliza.

However, Stead must have been very concerned that if the Salvation Army was forced to return Eliza to her family she would have a tale to tell that would reflect very badly on him. His belief that she had been sold would be no justification for subjecting her to indecent assault by a French abortionist. He had no rights over Eliza at all. The model he had concocted with Josephine Butler, that they would be buying a girl in the market as black slaves were bought and released by abolitionists in America, did not work. Instead of releasing Eliza they were holding her captive. In fact, they had abducted a perfectly innocent girl and, effectively, enslaved her. No wonder Stead was keeping his head down. But the writing was very soon on the wall.

Chapter Eight
A letter from Eliza

Mrs Armstrong had written to Eliza at the address in France given to her by Bramwell Booth in the presence of Inspector Borner. She perhaps had only a faint hope that she would get a reply. But on 14 August a letter arrived with a French post mark. The excitement at 32 Charles Street must have been intense. The letter began:

> "Dear Mother, I have received your nice letter, and I was glad that you are getting on all right. I cannot write myself good enough, so the young English governess is going to write for me."

The letter continued in the handwriting of the governess.

> "You must not be broken-hearted about me, for I am very comfortable indeed."

And then a last note written by Eliza:

> "Your loving child Eliza Armstrong. Write me soon, dear mother, Good-bye and bless you and my father."

The governess added a further note to reassure the Armstrongs that Eliza's was safe and comfortable.

They had finally found where Eliza was, and at the same time the government had taken a hand in the case. The Solicitor to the Treasury (the equivalent then of the Director of Public Prosecutions) appointed an officer called Charles Von Tornow to go to France and bring Eliza back. So that there would be no doubt about her identification and that she should be reassured she was coming home, her father Charles was asked to accompany Von Tornow. Sadly, no intimate account of the journey they made has ever been given.

What we do know is that they left London on 19 August and reached Loriol-sur-Drome two days later on 21 August. They were looking for the Monsieur Berard who lived at the address given to them by Bramwell Booth, but the house was locked up. Charles Armstrong and Von Turnow made enquiries and tracked the family down to a holiday place in the mountains. But Eliza was not with them. A few days earlier a letter had come from Bramwell Booth asking the Berard family to send Eliza back to Paris. There was nothing for Charles and the Inspector to do but head back to London disappointed and anxious—but not quite empty handed. They took from Monsieur Berard a letter that had been written to him in July by his sister, a Mrs Combe and delivered by his nephew Edouard:

"Dear Theodore, You will look for the arrival of Edouard (Mrs Combe's son), if that has not already taken place, with a little girl thirteen-years-old. I cannot, for prudence sake, give you at this moment an explanation of her circumstances, but she is a modest little girl, and if you do not take her in at this critical moment she will be lost body and soul. Take care of her, then, until I reclaim her.

Put her to whatever work you like, for she is handy and active, and you can let her go where you like, telling her that I am informed of her behaviour. If you require it, you will be compensated; but if you give her food in return for her work, and a little kindness, God will lay it to your account. Embrace my son for me, and send me news of him.

Say that she is a little servant, but not that it is the Army that got her for you. Edouard, your nephew, is not known as an officer. Try and obtain the *Pall Mall Gazette* of the past week, and you will see something that will astonish you immensely. Complete, my dear, the work I have commenced at any risk, and kindly shelter her. Fear nothing. Kisses to the dear ones—your affectionate Sister."

On the same day that Mrs Armstrong received her letter from Eliza the Criminal Law Amendment Bill was passed. To celebrate, meetings were called. One of the largest was scheduled for Friday 21st August at St James's Hall in Piccadilly, the day Inspector Von Tornow and Mr Armstrong arrived in Loriol. The distinguished representatives of many moral purity movements were on the platform and included Bramwell Booth and Stead. Most of the crowd that packed the Hall were their supporters, but one or two hecklers had infiltrated the celebratory throng and upset the proceedings by calling out: "Where's Eliza?" and "Where's Lizzie Armstrong?"

Stead was one of the last to speak. Stung by these taunts he finally let down his guard and harangued the tormentors. A stenographer took down his words verbatim:

"I will tell you about Armstrong. There is Mrs Booth standing here as the representative of the Salvation Army, who has been abused about Lizzie Armstrong, and I say that Mrs Booth and General Booth, and all the Salvation Army, who have been abused about Lizzie Armstrong, are as innocent of everything concerning taking that girl away as Mr Stansfield (an MP and member of the National Vigilance Association) is. They had absolutely nothing to do with it (loud applause).

I take some shame to myself that I have not taken an early opportunity of clearing the Salvation Army absolutely from all responsibility in the matter, and I alone, standing before you now; I am solely responsible for taking Lizzie Armstrong away from her mother's house. (loud applause). And I say this: that those good men and philanthropic strangers and others who are anxious to restore that child to her mother's house are taking upon themselves a responsibility greater by far than anything that the

Secret Commission of the *Pall Mall Gazette* ever took upon itself in the whole course of investigation.

We took that child from a place that was steeped in vice; from a mother who has admitted that she was going to a brothel as she thought, and instead of taking her to a brothel we placed her in good and Christian guardianship. (Great cheering). I ought to make on explanation; we did take that girl to a brothel for about half an hour; she did not know it was a brothel. She simply knew she was going to an hotel, but no suspicion or shadow of thought of anything wrong crossed that girl's mind; we took her there, and we took her away from there; we placed her in the hands of the Salvation Army who had absolutely nothing whatever to do with the taking her to the brothel afterwards."

So Stead was still defiant. However, he knew by then that Eliza was on her way back to England, not to her parents in Charles Street, but to the safety and comfort of his own home in Wimbledon. Bramwell Booth, under pressure from the police and now from the Treasury Solicitor, which had taken charge of the investigation, had been forced to bring Eliza out of hiding. There was a very real prospect now that those involved in what most of the newspapers referred to as the "abduction" of Eliza, would face prosecution and public humiliation. Whether or not Eliza went back to her mother, Inspector Borner would want to interview the girl.

Who, or what, it was that broke Stead's defiance in the face of mounting pressure for him to produce Eliza is not clear. A reporter from *Lloyd's Weekly* tried to convince him Mrs Armstrong really did want her child, and a Mr John Thicknesse of the Minors' Protection League had become involved, offering to act as a kind of broker. The negotiations which went on that weekend were like the final resolution of a kidnapping with those handing back their victim doing their best to limit the damage. Stead, just the day after he had declaimed emphatically that he had taken Eliza from a "place that was steeped in vice" sat at his desk and wrote out the following letter addressed to Mrs Armstrong. It began with a blatant lie:

> "I am informed to-day, for the first time, that you wish your daughter, Eliza, restored to you. She is well taken care of, and very happy; but, of course, if you and Mr Armstrong really want her returned to you I am, and always have been, ready to comply with your request. As yet however, you have not informed anyone with whom I have been in communication through the police or the Salvation Army people that you desire her to be taken from a good situation in order to have her back at home. If, however, you now inform me that you want to have her back, I shall deliver her over to you on receipt of your letter to that effect. I would suggest, however, that if you only wish to satisfy yourself that Eliza is all right and safe, that you and Mr Armstrong should see her for yourselves, and that then she should return to her situation, where she is giving good satisfaction and doing very well—I am yours, very truly THE CHIEF DIRECTOR".

Clearly Stead still believed that he had some legal hold over Eliza and that her mother would need to put her request that she be returned home in writing. Even at this late hour he seemed unaware that he was not entitled to strike a bargain with Mrs Armstrong and that whatever reply she might make would have no influence on Inspector Borner. Eliza was on her way back to England because the law had said she must be returned not because someone in the Salvation Army had decided it was the right thing to do. However, Stead had arranged for her to be delivered first to his own home in Wimbledon rather than to Charles Street. And he was keen to keep the long arm of the law at full stretch.

Police News

THE ILLUSTRATED LAW COURTS AND WEEKLY RECORD.

No. 1,125. SATURDAY, SEPTEMBER 5, 1885. Price One Penny.

THE CASE OF ELIZA ARMSTRONG — THE LOST CHILD.

THE FATHER. THE SISTER. NEW HEADING 32 CHARLES STREET MARYLEBONE. A YOUNGER MEMBER OF THE FAMILY. ELIZA ARMSTRONG. THE EXPECTED RETURN — SCENE OUTSIDE THE HOUSE.

Chapter Nine
Eliza's Return

When Eliza first arrived at the Stead's Wimbledon villa he spoke to her briefly and tried to persuade her to say that she would prefer to stay with the people who had adopted her. When she said she wanted to see her mother he left her in the care of his wife and prepared to take a well earned break from all the excitement of the past months. He was off to the resort of Gridenwald in the Swiss Alps once he had tied up things at the office. The letter he had written to Mrs Armstrong saying he had only just learned that she wanted Eliza back he left with his hired hand Sampson Jacques. Was he, perhaps, frightened of meeting Mrs Armstrong? Whatever the reason, Stead would not witness the reunion of the mother and the daughter he claimed she had sold for £5.

Mr Jacques was a shadowy figure whose role in the affair only came to light later on. Stead sometimes described him, anonymously in the Maiden Tribute articles, as his agent. Sampson Jacques was a false name adopted for the purposes of the Secret Commission. Not much is known about this man whose real name was, apparently, Mr Mussabini. For the rest of this story he will remain Sampson Jacques for reasons which will become clear.

Eliza spent the Saturday night, 22nd August, in Wimbledon. The following morning, Jacques and Mr Thicknesse, who had offered to act as a kind of broker in the hand over of Eliza, went to Charles Street. While Jacques kept watch at the end of the street, Mr Thicknesse once again asked Mrs Armstrong if she really wanted her daughter back. He now had the letter Stead had written and he asked her to read it. Mrs Armstrong said she had not changed her mind. At that Mr Thicknesse told Jacques of the decision and it was arranged that they would come to collect Mrs Armstrong the next morning, the Monday, at 10 am to take her to Wimbledon. But Jacques warned her that on no account should she tell anyone, especially the police, of this arrangement.

However, Mrs Armstrong had had enough of the threats and promises of Mr Booth and his friends and promptly contacted Inspector Borner, who was still in pursuit of Rebecca Jarrett. Borner arrived promptly in Charles Street the following morning and was already with Mrs Armstrong when Sampson Jacques and Mr Thicknesse arrived. They had never seen him before and were taken aback when he introduced himself. But there was nothing they could do but allow him to accompany them to Wimbledon. Eliza's elder sister went too, as moral support for her mother.

Borner had thought that Rebecca Jarrett might be at Stead's house and had arranged for plain clothes detectives to watch it. But when they arrived there was no sign of her, nor of Stead or Mr Booth. Emma, Stead's wife, greeted them cordially and showed them in. She shook hands with Mrs Armstrong when Jacques introduced her. She then left the room and returned with Eliza who threw herself into her mother's arms and kissed her elder sister. All three were in tears and Mrs Armstrong kept crying: "Oh my child!" Borner jotted down: "the child seemed very glad to see her mother, and the mother to see her child." Mrs Stead suggested that the three should be left alone for a while and they were shown into another room while Jacques and Mr Thicknesse wandered around the garden. After a while, Mrs Stead went to see Mrs Armstrong and returned to tell Mr Jacques:

"The mother is resolved to take the child home, and the girl is determined to go with her; they seem very firm on this." Reluctantly Jacques said: "Well then, we must let them go."

Stead's wife Emma treated Mrs Armstrong with a civility that must have surprised and pleased her. They had

75

lunch together, Eliza, her elder sister and her mother, Mr Thicknesse and Mr Jacques. What the conversation was we can only imagine: "More potatoes Mrs Armstrong?" "I wonder if you would mind passing the mustard." A servant was in attendance. Without Stead himself there the mood was perhaps quite relaxed. But he had arranged in his absence for some formalities to be completed before Mrs Armstrong was allowed to have her daughter back. With Mr Thickenesse, he had drafted a statement which he wanted Mrs Armstrong to sign acknowledging receipt of her daughter in mint condition. It read:

"I have received my daughter Eliza safe and sound, together with double the wages agreed on for all the time she has been away. My daughter tells me she has been very happy and comfortable. The people with whom she has been have been very kind to her, and I am quite satisfied she has been subjected to no outrage — signed Elizabeth Armstrong and witnessed by Mr William Thicknesse, Secretary of the Minor's Protection League"

Mrs Armstrong duly signed. Inspector Borner then took charge. Samson Jacques made one last effort to persuade Mrs Armstrong to leave Eliza in the "good company" which she had enjoyed since her abduction, but there was no question of that. Inspector Borner then announced that he was taking Eliza, her sister and mother to Scotland Yard to make statements. Sampson Jacques put a brave face on this news, telling Borner they wanted "all the publicity they could get." Borner, however, remained discreet. He made no public statement to the Press about where Eliza had been recovered.

That Monday night, news had got around in Lisson Grove that Eliza was at last coming home. An excited crowd had gathered outside 32 Charles Street and had to be kept in order by the police. For her own protection Eliza got out of the cab in nearby Devonshire Street and, according to the local newspaper, was put up for the night by a benevolent lady; presumably not the same well-wisher who had been mistaken for a procuress and beaten within an inch of her life. She stayed the night there, but on the following day, when Inspector Borner came to take her to Scotland Yard to make a statement, the crowds gathered again.

"On Tuesday morning, the excitement in Devonshire Street and neighbourhood was renewed," reported the *Marylebone Mercury*.

> "Numbers of persons assembled, and as it became known that the girl would in the course of the day be taken to Scotland Yard by detectives, the crowd kept increasing. In the forenoon, two detectives arrived in a cab, and Eliza Armstrong and her mother were taken to the chief Metropolitan Police Station at Whitehall. Large numbers of persons followed the cab through Lisson Grove and along the Marylebone road, anxious to obtain a sight of the child who had been the subject of so much romantic adventure."

Most newspaper accounts of Eliza's dramatic homecoming were fiercely critical of those who had abducted her. The *Pall Mall Gazette* took a more sanguine view. Nobody had asked for the return of Eliza, according to their story, until the previous Friday. Then she had been promptly returned to her mother, and the letter she had signed as a kind of moral "receipt" for her daughter was published, without her permission. As far as the *Gazette* was concerned, all was well that ended well. Their report stated:

> "Eliza has grown a good deal since she left England and her mother expressed herself as much pleased at the improvement in her appearance. Eliza herself spoke in the most grateful manner of Mrs Sullivan (Rebecca Jarrett) and laughed at the idea that any harm had been done to her."

There followed a letter Eliza had written to Katie Booth, the eldest daughter of William and Catherine Booth, founders of the Salvation Army. Katie Booth had been one of the founders of the first Army outpost in Paris where she became known as La Marechale. When Eliza was in Paris, Katie Booth had been responsible for her. The *Gazette* wanted its readers to know how fond Eliza had become of one of her captors. Again, the letter was published without consulting Eliza:

"Dear Marechal, I love you very much. You are a kind lady. I thank you very much for that nice present you sent to me. I was very happy here. The girls was so kind to me. I was very fond of going to the meetings. I likes it very much. I hope I shall go to London to see my dear mother and father and the lady that fetched me here. Will you be so kind has to fetch me one of my likeness (a photo) to give to my mother. She will be so please to have it. I hope the lord takes me and Fanny in his arms, takeing care of us till we have got to the journey. Good bye and God bless, for my sake, My dear Marechal—Eliza Armstrong."

In contrast, the *Marylebone Mercury* published the widespread view that Eliza and her mother had been treated with utter contempt by Stead and the Salvation Army:

"The impudence of these people is immeasurable.. Many of us know what terrible anxiety preys upon a parent when a child is lost for only a few hours. Multiply that by days and weeks and then conceive what mental suffering must have been inflicted upon the mother of Eliza Armstrong. Such considerations of course do not weigh with a sensational journalist or with the rattler of a religious begging-box... One of the worst features in this discreditable story is the absence of any sense of moral obligation on behalf of the chief actors. They are a law unto themselves."

Stead, enjoying the Alpine air in Grindelwald, still believed himself to be in the clear and was apparently unconcerned about the consequences of Eliza's return. But he was not long into his sojourn when he learned that the law took a more prosaic view of what was right and what was wrong. The chief witness, Eliza herself, had told her story and the lady who had befriended her, Rebecca Jarrett (aka "Mrs Sullivan") was in deep trouble.

Chapter Ten
The long arm of the law

At the time Stead was on his way to Grindelwald in the Swiss Alps he had no idea a warrant had been issued for the arrest of Rebecca Jarrett. He had never intended when he wrote the Maiden Tribute account of "the girl of thirteen bought for £5" that Jarrett would be exposed to public censure. He had not named her. And it does not seem to have occurred to him that anybody would ever discover who 'Lily' really was. He had arranged for her to disappear as if she were a little harlot lost in the London labyrinth. Although he could no longer deny that he and Jarrett had been involved in taking Eliza and handing her over to the Salvation Army, he was still trying to argue that she was just one girl among several involved in his investigations and that she was only in part the 'Lily' of his story. But which part?

Three days after the issue of the warrant for the arrest of Jarrett she was still missing. On 29 August, Inspector Borner and another police officer went to see Bramwell Booth at the Queen Victoria Street headquarters of the Salvation Army. They asked if he could tell them where Jarrett was. "Yes", Booth told them. "but perhaps it would be best that I should have her brought to London on Monday." Inspector Borner said he could save Booth the trouble and expense if he simply gave him an address. Booth refused and said he preferred to have Jarrett brought to London. He then asked: "What do you want her for?"

Borner told him that Jarrett had said Mrs Armstrong had sold her child, but the mother denied it. To which Booth replied: "It was Mrs Broughton that had the money," referring to Mrs Armstrong's friend and neighbour. "She denied it, too", said Borner.

It must have been very confusing for Bramwell Booth who had everything third hand from Jarrett and Stead. Booth was led to believe that the "procuress" was Nancy Broughton who had the bulk of the money from Jarrett, but that Mrs Armstrong did know her daughter was being sold to a brothel. It was irrelevant, anyway, as far as Borner was concerned. He wanted Jarrett.

Rebecca duly gave herself up at Scotland Yard. Inspector Borner then made further inquiries, piecing together the events of the day Eliza was taken away from Charles Street. Accompanied by Eliza, he retraced her steps on the day after Derby Day and the following morning. She was able to identify the place she was first taken to, the house in Milton Street where her parents had been with the *Lloyd's Weekly* reporter (and where her father had caused such a stir in his working clothes), and then a place in Poland Street, off Oxford Street, evidently the brothel mentioned in the Maiden Tribute article, where she had been taken by Jarrett and put to bed. Finally, Eliza showed Borner a place she had been to near Harley Street which did not seem to be mentioned in the original story. Stead had his reasons for this omission, as was to become clear later.

The evidence collected by Borner led to the issue of warrants for the arrest of Stead, Samson Jacques, a French accoucheuse or midwife called Madame Mourez, Bramwell Booth, Chief of Staff of the Salvation Army and a Mrs Combe, also of the Army. On 2nd September, Rebecca Jarrett alone appeared in the dock at Bow Street Magistrates Court charged with four offences. There were two separate charges relating to the abduction of Eliza, a charge of indecent assault and another of administering a noxious substance. The Magistrate was told that Stead was abroad but that a telegram would be sent immediately to instruct him to return. That night the defiant reply came in by telegraph dated 'Grindelwald, Wednesday night, September 2':

81

"THE ARREST OF REBECCA JARRETT IS OF A PIECE WITH THE CITY SOLICITOR'S PROSECUTION OF THE NEWSBOYS. I ALONE AM RESPONSIBLE. REBECCA JARRETT WAS ONLY MY UNWILLING AGENT. I AM RETURNING BY THE FIRST EXPRESS TO CLAIM THE SOLE RESPONSIBILITY FOR THE ALLEGED ABDUCTION, AND TO DEMAND, IF CONDEMNED, THE SOLE PUNISHMENT. MEANWHILE I AM DELIGHTED AT THE OPPORTUNITY THUS AFFORDED ME OF PUBLICLY VINDICATING THE PROCEEDINGS OF THE SECRET COMMISSION"

One by one members of the Secret Commission who were directly involved with Eliza's disappearance were issued with a summons to appear at Bow Street on 7th September to answer the charges against them. Bramwell Booth and a Mrs Combe faced prosecution for their part in the abduction. Who was Mrs Combe? It was she who had written the letter to her brother in France asking him to take Eliza as a servant and to keep quiet about the involvement of the Salvation Army. The charge of indecent assault and administering a noxious substance was made against Rebecca Jarrett, Sampson Jacques and a Madame Mourez, evidently the French woman who had been tracked down to Milton Street by *Lloyd's Weekly* and, later, by Inspector Borner. Stead faced all the charges: abduction, indecent assault and administering a noxious substance.

In the few days he had after his return from the Swiss Alps, Stead had managed to put together a 'defence fund' of more than £600 (around £35,000 at today's prices) to pay for lawyers. Each member of the now not-so-secret Commission had their legal representative, apart from Stead himself. He retained a legal adviser but was determined to be his own representative.

On the morning of Monday 7th September 1885, an excited crowd gathered outside Bow Street Police Court, opposite the Opera House in Covent Garden. A little before 11am the doors of the imposing new building were eased open, and there was an unseemly scrum for seats in the public gallery. As well as the general public, who did not want to miss what promised to be a fascinating drama, there were some very respectable ladies attending to learn the fate of their friends and husbands who were standing trial. One or two were in the distinctive uniform of the Salvation Army, and they suffered some ugly looks from those in the public gallery.

After the first day's full sitting, the *Daily News* gave a description of the atmosphere in court:

> "The applications for bail having been duly settled, the defendants left their places in front of the dock to proceed to the office, whereupon those at the back of the court raised a perfect howl of execration at them as they passed from the court into the passage beyond. The court, however, was promptly cleared, but the excitement of the large mob which had gathered in the street outside was not to be appeased."

The police had to smuggle some of the defendants out to avoid the angry crowd. Jarrett had been granted bail and was allowed to leave by the magistrate's private door which was out of sight of the main entrance to the court. Mrs Combe got away in a hansom cab unrecognised. Following closely was a four wheeled cab in which Stead was spotted, along with some companions, and was jeered. According to the *Daily News*:

> "The storm, however, had apparently been brewing more especially for Mr Bramwell Booth, and it is a fortunate thing for him that he drove out of the same shelter whilst the crowd was broken from the passage of the previous cab. Although the glass was down he was soon espied and a chase after the vehicle ensued. By the aid of the short start he had obtained and a swift horse he managed to turn into the Strand

> before his pursuers caught him up, the heavy traffic in that thoroughfare rendering any pursuit on foot futile."

While the real Bramwell Booth made his escape, the man who had worked so hard to reunite Eliza with her mother took the rap.

> "A curious incident, showing the feelings of the crowd, occurred to Mr Catling, the editor of *Lloyd's News*. Being tall, and wearing a black suit, some person stated that he was 'General' Booth and he was hustled with considerable violence."

When the committal proceedings began, Rebecca Jarrett, the only defendant who had been kept in custody, was led to the dock by two gaolers amidst hissing in the public gallery and mutterings of "That's her!". The other defendants answering to their names came in, as the *Gazette* put it, "Indian File": Mr. Stead, Mr. Bramwell Booth, Mr. Jacques, Mdme. Combe, and Mdme. Mourez. They stood and then sat in a narrow area in front of the dock with Mr Booth aiming his enormous ear-trumpet at whoever was speaking. There was just a tantalising glimpse of Eliza, her mother and other witnesses for the prosecution before they were ushered out of court and leading the prosecution, Mr Poland Q.C. began a long account of the whole affair. For the first time, members of the public and journalists from rival newspapers learned what had really happened to Eliza. This, in its detail, was fascinating, and to many, shocking, enough. But the one person everyone wanted to hear from was little Eliza herself, the thirteen year old supposedly sold to a brothel by her mother.

According to the *Daily Telegraph* report, the accused looked quite relaxed during Mr Poland's two-hour opening speech.

> "Mrs Combe, a diminutive woman, attired in the conventional dress of the Salvation Army, maintained a cheerful demeanour throughout, but, unlike her,

Madame Mourez appeared to feel her position acutely, the more so, as being a foreigner, she clearly did not understand the exact purport of all that was going on... Mr Stead, who was apparently regarded as the chief of the accused parties, followed the proceedings with close attention, and took copious notes, while his 'fidus Achates' (intimate companion), as the prosecuting counsel termed Mr Jacques, assumed the aspect of a man amused rather than alarmed."

Rebecca Jarrett, said the report, at first seemed to regard the matter lightly, but "later on, when the chief witness was produced, she became evidently concerned, and for some time leaned on the dock-rail with her handkerchief to her face."

Just before he went off on holiday to Switzerland, and when Eliza had been reunited with her mother, Stead had written a piece for the *Pall Mall Gazette* which was a kind of apologia for what he had done. It was published on 25th August and afforded the prosecutor Mr Poland, in his opening speech at Bow Street, an opportunity to illustrate to the magistrate the manner in which the editor misled his readers with versions of events which did not tally with what had, in fact, taken place. Mr Poland had read from the *Gazette*:

> "It was no part of our original intention to mention any names, and but for the intervention of fussy ignorance and unworthy jealousy, none of the persons of whose injured feelings so much has been heard would ever have suffered a single pang. That owing to such intervention even the humblest of the dwellers in Marylebone should have experienced even a moment's uneasiness no one regrets more than myself.
>
> At the outset of our inquiry we were informed that children of twelve and thirteen were procured by brothel keepers and decoy girls, examined by midwives,

taken to brothels, and there drugged or intoxicated, and violently outraged. One case in particular of a child just under thirteen who was ruined by force in a certain brothel—she shrieking in vain the while for her mother, and crying to be taken home—came before us, but it was a matter of evidence not of knowledge.

In order to verify the possibility and the facility with which such crimes could be committed, I was at that early stage in the inquiry compelled to employ an agent in whose present integrity I firmly believe, but who had at one time kept a brothel in Marylebone"

Mr. Poland interjected: "I do not know if this is intended for Jarrett. We shall probably hear hereafter."

Mr. Russell (representing Rebecca): "Certainly it is intended for Jarrett."

Mr Poland continued reading from the *Gazette*:

"... but who had at one time kept a brothel in Marylebone, and was believed by her old friends still to be living a life of sin. If it were to be done again I should have no need to use an agent. I could tomorrow buy a child twelve years of age direct from her mother for £4, and get a written receipt certifying that she was sold for prostitution; but at that time I was a novice, and had to rely upon agents."

At this point in his sardonic recitation, Mr. Poland appealed directly to the packed public gallery at Bow Street, with good effect.

"I should consider Mr. Stead a very credulous man indeed, if he believes that there is an English mother in poor circumstances who would sell her child for prostitution, and give a receipt certifying what she had done. They might trick the mother, as they did in this case; but as to there being any mothers, either in the upper or middle classes, who are prepared to sell their children for that purpose, I would not believe it. I have some experience of vice in the metropolis, and I believe it is a foul libel to say and print that any English mother among people would sell her children for such a purpose."

There was loud cheering and the magistrate, Mr Vaughan, had to quell the hubbub which ensued. Mr Poland then continued to quote Stead:

> "My agent, who had no monetary interest in the matter, and was pressed most unwillingly into the service, to make some atonement for the crimes she had committed in her past life by exposing the method of procuration and seduction, informed me, after making inquiries, that she knew where she could buy a girl of thirteen for £4."

Mr. Poland: "He had a suspicion that she had got possession of the child by fraud. What she told Mr. Stead we shall see afterwards."

> "The bargain was £3 down and £2 after examination by a midwife had proved her to be all right. I was told that the bargain was not made direct with the mother, but through the intermediary of a neighbour. As I only wanted the child in order to enable me to verify the facts already reported to me, of the ease with which procuration, certification, drugging, and rape could be accomplished, and then to rescue her from what appeared to be most demoralizing surroundings, I consented. I paid £1 down on the day of delivery, and subsequently gave £2 for transmission to Charles-street."

Mr. Poland: "The mother never saw the child after she was taken away that afternoon. The payment of the £3 was fiction, the £2 was fiction; in fact, the whole thing was fiction."

> "The girl was brought to me (Mr. Stead) as stated."

Mr. Poland: "That is, to Albany-street, where he was with the young lady."

"She knew nothing about it, believing, as all girls similarly procured do, that she was going to a situation. She was right in that belief; but before she went to her situation she was taken first to the midwife, and then to the identical brothel where the little girl had been outraged, of whom I have spoken, and who so far as the outrage is concerned, is the original of 'Lily'."

Mr. Poland: "If the story in the *Pall Mall Gazette* is all true as to this child not being Lily, but some other child, this is as devoid of reality and is as much fiction as the other story is."

"She smelt the chloroform bottle, and dozed off into a gentle slumber, from which unfortunately she woke with a start when I entered the room to see that she was really asleep."

Mr. Poland: "He enters the girl's room, and the girl cried, 'There's a man in the room,' and he went out again."

"I instantly disappeared, and she said the other day that she thought it was all a dream."

Mr. Poland "She says it was not a dream. She has a very vivid recollection of everything that occurred."

"After remaining there half an hour, she was taken to the house of a respectable lady"—

Mr. Poland: "We cannot get the address of that respectable lady, but we hope to find her"—

"...where she slept, and next morning I sent her off to France, where she was placed in a situation by the Salvation Army. The girl was kept quite ignorant about everything and was much attached to my agent —'a very kind lady,' so she told me on Sunday, 'whom I would like to see again'."

Mr. Poland: "The very kind lady was Jarrett, whom she had only seen two or three days in Paris."

Mr. Waddy (representing Bramwell Booth): "The very kind lady was Mdme. Combe."

Mr. Poland: "I think you are wrong; the lady referred to was Jarrett."

Mr. Stead: "Mr. Poland is right."

"Excepting the momentary surprise…"

Mr. Poland: "Surprise! indecently assaulted"

"… of the midwife's examination, which was necessary to prove that a little harlot had not been palmed off upon us, she experienced not the slightest inconvenience. It will be seen from the above that 'Lily' was not Eliza Armstrong."

Mr. Poland: "Demonstrating she was. The quotation from the letter proves it",

"—but that we took her all unwitting over the ground up to the very point at which another poor girl had actually been outraged before we picked her off the streets."

Mr. Poland: " 'Took her off the streets!' Defrauded the mother of her by fraud and false representations. That is what is called 'picking her off the streets', as if she was a little baby found."

"In no other way could we have proved by our own personal knowledge that a midwife would certify for immoral purposes, would sell chloroform for drugging the victim, or that a brothel keeper would allow a child so young to be admitted to her premises for purposes of violation. I may say that I kept personal watch over the girl from the time she left the midwife until she was safely home for the night, and that nothing could exceed the care which was taken to avoid suggesting any impure thought to the child's mind, who has now been restored to her mother, safe, sound, and much improved both in appearance and condition."

Whereas Stead had boldly printed stories of abduction and violation of young girls in the Maiden Tribute articles, in describing what had occurred during his own mock abduction of Eliza, he had become rather precious. He knew very well that Mdme Mourez had lifted up the girl's skirt and inserted her finger, or fingers, in her vagina. This, he imagined, was the only time Eliza had experienced "the slightest inconvenience". Neither, apparently, had Rebecca Jarrett's attempt to administer chloroform bothered Eliza much. Nor, for that matter, the terrible anxiety she had suffered in Poland Street when she heard the voice of a man in the room, though he had written her startled cry into his story as if it were one of real anguish.

And Stead had left out of his account an episode which was not uncovered until the Bow Street proceedings were already underway. Mr Booth was able to assure Mrs Armstrong that Eliza had not been "outraged", and had a certificate to prove it, because, after she left Poland Street, Eliza had been examined again, this time by an eminent doctor who, for a fee of three guineas, had her chloroformed while asleep and slipped his expert finger into her vagina so that he could pronounce her *virgo intacta*. Eliza knew nothing of this episode as she had been rendered oblivious by a nurse in the "respectable home" to which Stead had taken her.

By the time Mr Poland had finished his opening speech it was clear that Stead had doctored his story to a considerable extent. He was still trying to convince the magistrates that Eliza was not really the 'Lily' of the Maiden Tribute, and he would hang on to that fiction for some time, even though, at Bow Street he was confronted by Eliza as the chief witness for the prosecution.

Chapter Eleven
Eliza tells her story

It was late in the day when Eliza made her appearance. She began to give her evidence from the witness box, but her voice was so slight she had to be called down and given a seat directly in front of the defendants. She was wearing a greyish brown cape which Rebecca Jarrett had bought her, and a large straw Duchess of Devonshire hat, heavily trimmed, with a woollen comforter encircling her neck. As Mr Poland led her through her story she answered questions put to her with a touching directness, and the court-room hung on every word.

Eliza remembered being called in to see Mrs Broughton and being told that her friend Mrs Sullivan was looking for a servant girl. She thought Mrs Sullivan said she lived in Wimbledon. Eliza was told she would have to do the scrubbing because Mrs Sullivan could not kneel. She went home to ask her mother if she could go and her mother said: "No". That was on 2nd June, but the next day her mother changed her mind. Eliza was very keen to take the job. Mrs Armstrong said that if Eliza was to go away to service she would need some new clothes. What she had on was worn and ragged. Mrs Sullivan said she would buy Eliza some new clothes as her "husband was a very particular man."

In court Mrs Sullivan was always referred to by her real name, Rebecca Jarrett.

> "She first bought me a pair of boots at Chandler's, in Marylebone. The boots were taken back to Mrs. Broughton's, where I put them on. I afterwards took Mrs. Jarrett to a clothes shop (Davis's) in Edgware-road, where she bought me a new frock, and she bought a hat at Thompson's, also a necktie and scarf. We then went back to Broughton's, where I put off my old things and put on the new things. I then went

home, when I had dinner with my father and mother, Mrs. Sullivan remaining at Broughton's. This was about half-past two o'clock. We started at three o'clock. When I left home mother was against the door, and she said she would come and see me before I went off. She went round to the school to give my brother the key of the house to hold while she went to see me off."

That was the last time Eliza saw her mother before they were re-united at the end of August. Her memory about going home to lunch with her mother and her father was questioned. She really could not remember. When she went off with Jarrett to the omnibus, Mrs Broughton came with them. They went in a roundabout way to Albany Street which is on the opposite side of Regents Park from Lisson Grove. There she met a young lady and a man she did not know and did not give his name. But she could identify him now. Stead was asked to stand in court. They all had had tea together.

After tea Jarrett took Eliza out to buy some more clothes, which she changed into in Albany Street. The other woman who was there said Eliza should have her hair "frizzed up" but Eliza said "Mother would not allow it" so nothing was done. After a while Jarrett and the other lady took Eliza in a handsome cab to another place. She heard Jarrett give the address as Milton Street, Dorset Square. When they got there she noticed a man waiting outside, who she did not know. (This was Samson Jacques, a *Pall Mall Gazette* journalist). They all went into the place where she met a French woman. This was Madame Mourez who duly stood up in court to be identified. Madame Mourez took her into a room on her own and lifted up her skirts. Eliza struggled and tried to get away. But she did not cry out. When she went back into the room where Jarrett was she said: "She is a dirty woman".

There was some discussion between Jarrett, the man and Madame Mourez. Then they left and there was a four-wheeled cab waiting outside. She and Jarrett got in, but not the man. Eliza did not hear the address given to the cabman but she knew now they had gone to Poland Street. The cab stopped outside a ham and beef shop. Jarrett got out to get some change to pay for the cab.

"Me and Mrs. Sullivan walked up the street, and these two men followed us. We went into a house next door to the ham and beef shop, and the two men did so too. The two gentlemen went in first—into a back room upstairs, on the first floor. Jarrett and I then went upstairs into the front room on the same floor, which was a bedroom."

Eliza by this time had no idea what was going on. Jarrett had told her they would stay there the night, then go to Wimbledon the next day. The "lady of the house" in Poland Street came in followed by the two men, who had drinks. Eliza thought it was whiskey. She was given a glass of lemonade. Then Jarrett gave her a book to look at with pictures in it. After a while Jarrett told her to get undressed and get into bed.

Led by Mr Poland, Eliza came to the crux of her story, the incident which Stead, in his version of events in the *Pall Mall Gazette* told with such drama.

"You undressed and went to bed?—Yes. I asked Jarrett if she were going to bed too. She said she was waiting for the young lady to come.

What was she doing when you undressed and went to bed?—She was looking at a book.

Can you tell what time it was then?—No.

Did Mrs. Jarrett then come to bed?—Yes; but she did not undress—she only laid down alongside of me on the bed.

Did she do anything to you?—She put something on a handkerchief—I could not see what it was.

What did she do with the handkerchief?—Put it up to my nose.

Did you smell anything?—Yes, a funny smell. Did she say anything when she gave you this?—She said it was scent.

Did she say what you were to do?—She said, 'Give it a good sniff up.'

What did you do after the handkerchief was put to your nose?—I threw the handkerchief by the side of the bed.

Where had she put the handkerchief?—Upon my nose.

Did you sniff it or not?—Yes. Mrs. Jarrett then got up, and I then heard somebody at the door, which was open.

Did anybody come in?—Yes, sir.

Did you see who came in?—There were curtains all around the bed, and I could not see. You were undressed in bed at this time?—Yes.

What did you do?—I could hear a voice, and I could tell it was a man's voice

What did you do?—I screamed out; I said, 'There is a man in the room.' Jarrett said, 'What is the matter?' I heard a man go out.

Then she said to you, 'What is the matter?'—Yes.

What did you say?—I said, 'There is a man in the room.'

And she put the curtain up, and said, 'Why, there is no man in the room.' I said, 'No, because he was gone out of the room.' She then left the room. She was not away long."

This, then, was the true story of Lily's violation as told in the *Pall Mall Gazette*. She could have been raped, of course. Stead had Eliza entirely at his mercy, despite Jarrett's inexpert fumbling with the chloroform which was tossed away. She had been indecently assaulted by the

French woman on his instructions and she was now in a brothel in her night-clothes. She was bewildered and upset and nobody told her what was going on. The only person she knew at all was Jarrett whose home she imagined she would go to, eventually. But she did not stay the night in Poland Street. Jarrett had gone out of the room leaving Eliza alone after the scare about the man coming in. Eliza continued with her story:

> "When she came back she said, 'Get up and dress yourself, because there are too many men in the house.' We then dressed ourselves—Jarrett putting on her hat and jacket—and we went out, going away in a four-wheel cab, which was at the door. A man got on the box—it was the other man, not Jacques. I cannot describe that man. I heard no directions given to the cabman. It was very late, but I cannot tell the hour when we left the house in Poland-street. We drove a long way, but I cannot tell the direction in which the cab went. We stopped at a large house, but we did not get out. The man on the box went into the house. We were kept waiting there about an hour, when the man came out at last saying it was 'all right, we could go in there for the night.' Mrs. Jarrett had not said anything to me while we were waiting. Jarrett and I went in, while the man went away. We went into a bedroom, and we went to bed. This was some time after midnight, I think. She told me I would go to her house the next morning."

While she was having breakfast the next morning Eliza was introduced to a woman she had not seen before, a Madame Combe, who was now seated in front of the dock. Madame Combe was asked to rise so that Eliza could identify her.

> "Did Mdme. Combe say anything to you?—She asked me if I would like to go to service. I said 'No' at first. Mdme. Combe and Mrs. Sullivan then went into a

room by themselves. I was at this time sitting crying. After some time they came back and sat down without saying anything. Then Mr. Stead came in and told us to come down, the cab was ready."

They all went to a railway station, but Eliza did not know which one. She had no idea where they were taking her until she got to Paris. She was put into the care of Catherine 'Katie' Booth, who had introduced the French to the Salvation Army in 1879 and endured, with another officer, Florence Soper, a series of violent attacks. Florence later married Catherine's brother Bramwell, who was now before the magistrates at Bow Street. Eliza did not say much about her stay in Paris, except that she went out with the girls selling the Salvation Army *War Cry* on the streets, a story which brought a roar of laughter from the public gallery. Jarrett travelled with Eliza to Paris but then left after two or three days saying she was going back to England to "get the house ready for her."

Meanwhile, as a dutiful daughter, Eliza had insisted that she should be allowed to write to her mother. She knew her address which she put on the envelope correctly: Mrs Armstrong, 32 Charles Street, Lisson Grove, Marylebone, London. When the letter was read out in court another mystery arising from the story of the child bought for £5 was solved.

Eliza had written:

"My dear Mother—I right these few lines to you hopping you are quite well. I am very happy. I have got a good home. I got good cloveing. I am in france. I goes in the park every night give my love to my brothers and sisters don't fret about I as plenty to eat. They are very kind to I like the place very much. I am going to another place soon. I will come and see you soon as I can. How is little Charley gitting on. I hope you are gitting on. I am a good girl, they likes me very much. How is Miss Woodworth giting on. That all I got to say at preasant.

> As I was lying in my bed,
> some little forths gave in my head
> I forth of one, I forth of two,
> But most of all I forth of you"

So this was how Stead was able describe how little Lily did not spell very well. He had not only stolen the letter Eliza had written to her mother from Paris he had woven it into his story for bathetic affect.

Eliza's evidence at Bow Street was all too brief. She recalled being told by Mrs Combe that she was to go to a new place and that Mrs Combe's son had taken her to a place called Loriol in another part of France where she became the servant of a family which had an English governess. She had to work hard, but she was not ill-treated. She had written to her mother with the help of Miss Fielder the governess. After a while the family went away and she was left to look after the house in Loriol with other servants. One day she was told she was going back to Paris. When she realised she was going to be taken by two young men she began to cry. She went first to Valence in the Rhone Valley where they spent the night in a Salvation Army hostel, then back to Paris for a few days. She was finally taken back to England and Mr Stead's house in Wimbledon by a Miss Green of the Army.

On the Sunday night that she arrived, Mr Stead had talked to her in the garden. He had asked her if she had been sick on the sea crossing. He wanted to know of she would agree to go to a good situation. Eliza said she would like to ask her mother. She stayed the night and the next day she was in the garden when Mr Jacques asked if she would like to see her mother and she said: "Oh yes, very much so". And that, more or less, was the end of her story, though parts of it would be questioned in cross-examination.

Chapter Twelve
The drunken mother of Charles Street

The contrast between little Eliza, decked out in middle-class clothes provided for her by her captors and her mother, head in scarf and roughly dressed was striking when Mrs Armstrong took the stand. For the prosecution, Mr Poland took her through the to-ings and fro-ings in Charles Street on 2nd and 3rd June without much trouble, though she answered curtly and was clearly uneasy in the courtroom. In effect, Rebecca Jarrett and Stead had put her on trial, accusing her of letting Eliza go knowing full well that she was "wanted for a gentleman" and would be raped in a brothel. Mrs Armstrong would have none of that and stated forcefully that she knew Mrs Broughton not as a close friend but a close neighbour and trusted her. It was on Mrs Broughton's say so that she had let Eliza go, as she thought, into service. She was not given £1 for Eliza but she did take sixpence and bought something for the baby.

It was when first Eliza, and then Mrs Armstrong herself, were cross examined by Jarrett's counsel, Mr Russell, that the calm of the courtroom was broken. Eliza had got her story all mixed up and had to agree that some of things she had said she witnessed she had been told by her mother. In her account of the events of Derby Day she had thought her father had seen her in her new clothes but she now said he had not. Mr Russell, warming to his task, began to draw a picture of the poor little ragged girl freshly decked out in fine new clothes, well fed and cared for, quite the little lady. Eliza herself, frustratingly vague about some of the more pertinent details about what went on, proved herself to be sharply observant when it came to shopping.

Mr Russell: "Then you were taken out to get clothes. You were taken to various places for the clothes. To begin with, you got outside clothing. A frock?—Yes, sir.

A hat, which was not trimmed, but ribbon to trim it?—Yes.

Was it a smart hat?—Yes, sir.

Boots?—Yes.

And a scarf or necktie?—Yes.

Then the same day you got a complete change of underclothing? Or, in fact, your clothes were entirely new? They cost a good deal of money, child?—Yes.

Two or three or four pounds? Do you know what they cost?—No, sir. The boots was 3s.11d. (Laughter.)

Mr. Russell: You saw Mrs. Sullivan pay for the articles? Oh, well, I have the price of them, and I will see whether you are correct. I am told the boots were 4s.6d.

Witness: Three and elevenpence halfpenny. (Laughter.)

Mr. Russell: You tried on several pairs?

Witness: I think the frock was 8s. 6d. (Laughter.)

Mr. Russell: It was of a dark maroon colour. Oh! you have it on. Well, I am told that was 9s. 11d. (Laughter.) These figures may not be accurate. They are only from recollection. A hat, one and elevenpence halfpenny, and the trimmings cost a good deal more than the hat. Then you had the underclothing, and the day before you started the cloak you are now wearing. After you had got this clothing you were a bright, smart-looking girl, and quite pleased with yourself?—Yes, sir.

And you went back home, did you not, to show off your finery?—Yes."

Mr Russell's inference was that Mrs Armstrong must have realised that something odd was going on seeing her daughter dressed up in this way and all the money spent on her. He was also trying to get some kind of a straight answer to the question of whether her father had seen her smartened up. But she was not drawn. Neither was she prepared to agree that her mother was frequently drunk.

Having witnessed her daughter's cross-examination, Mrs Armstrong was in a fiery mood when Mr Russell began to question her evidence. He began to cast doubt on her account of how she had first begun to think that the Lily in the *Gazette* story might be Eliza.

Mr Russell: When did you first become uneasy about her?—When I got the *Gazette*.

That was about a month after she had gone?—Yes.

Mr. Russell: The *Pall Mall Gazette's* article was dated July 6th. You don't yourself ordinarily read the *Pall Mall Gazette*?—No, I never read it before or since.

Some neighbours called your attention to it?—Yes.

Who was the neighbour?—Mrs. Featherstone, who lived opposite me.

Had you known her long?—For many years.

Had you previous to that any anxiety about your child? —Yes, because I had not heard of her.

But you have just said you were first anxious when you saw the *Gazette*?—That made me more anxious.

Then you wish to correct that answer?—Of course I do.

Why of course?—Because I do. (Shouting in a loud voice.) Well, you are not going to baffle me. You are not going to cross-examine me as you have done my child. (Applause at the back of the court.)

Mr. Vaughan (The Magistrate): Just keep yourself quiet and answer the question.

Mrs. Armstrong: Am I bound to answer these questions?

Mr. Vaughan: Yes; keep yourself quiet, and quietly answer the questions, and be careful to consider the answers you give.

"Mr. Russell: It might perhaps be as well to let Mrs. Armstrong go on in her own way. It is no pleasure to me, Mrs. Armstrong, to put to you these questions, but I have to do it. You told me in answer to my first question as to when you first began to be anxious about your child that it was when you read the *Gazette*. Do you wish to correct that?—I was anxious before, but I was more anxious then."

What Mr Russell was driving at, as Mrs Armstrong well knew, was that she had not made the connection between Eliza's disappearance and the Maiden Tribute herself but had been put up to it by neighbours, some of whom were accusing her of having sold her daughter. For Mr Russell, all the fuss she made in trying to get Eliza back was simply an attempt to save face in Charles Street. Then Mr Russell began on the subject of Mrs Armstrong's 'character' which got the public gallery at Bow Street going, laughing and cheering as their champion gave as good as she got.

  "You have been in trouble once or twice, have you not?—In trouble for what?

  Well, you know what I mean.—I have never been a prostitute and never a thief. As for anything else, I can stand to it, and you can ask me.

  Well, I want you to tell me.—Well, what do you want? I'll tell you. (Laughter.)

  Have you been charged with an assault?—Yes; a good many years ago upon my sister-in-law, and I would do it again if she pulled my hair.

  Have you been charged with drunkenness?—Very likely I have; but I have never been in prison.

  Have you been fined?—I have, and paid it. (Laughter.)

  Your husband has paid it?—He might have done; it was very kind of him if he did. It has nothing to do with this case what I have done (vehemently), and I'm going to answer any further questions, and there you are. (Cheers from the back of the court.)

Mr. Vaughan: I cannot allow this.

Mr. Russell: It is very nearly time, your worship. It is to be hoped that the crowd at the back are not to be the judges in this matter. (To witness): Have you been charged and fined for using obscene language in the streets?—Oh, I often swear. (Laughter.)

Mr Russell: On the day your child left her home on the 3rd of June were you taken up drunk in the streets with your baby in your arms?—No; I were not.

Were you fined the next day?—Yes; all through my husband abusing me. It was all through this case, for letting the child go. That has nothing to do with this case. (To Mr. Vaughan): Am I bound to answer these questions?"

(Mr Armstrong had admitted that he had hit his wife when she was unable to tell him where Eliza had gone to.)

"Mr. Vaughan: Just preserve your temper and answer the questions quietly."

As each of the defendants had counsel representing them, and all wanted to make their points, Mrs Armstrong had to endure a lengthy cross-examination which continued into the third and fourth days of the Bow Street hearings. The public gallery was with her and several times Mr Vaughan had to call for order, losing his own temper on one occasion. One revelation which Stead and others thought extremely suspicious was that the Mr Thomas who had befriended her had on various occasions given her money: a half-crown here, five shillings there. When Mrs Armstrong asked what this was for she simply said:

"For telling him,"

which brought another burst of laughter. It was a belief in Stead's camp that Mrs Armstrong had been got at by opponents of the Criminal Law Amendment Act and persuaded to kick up a fuss about Eliza.

As Stead had chosen to defend himself, the time came for him to have an opportunity to cross examine Mrs Armstrong. It was not the first time they had set eyes on each other, but it was the first time they had spoken to each other since he had damned her as an uncaring, drunken mother. If the public gallery was anticipating a fierce confrontation they were disappointed. Stead was careful not to be aggressive and put his questions, deeply insulting though they were, in a contrite manner. He asked her if Rebecca Jarrett had not made it clear to her that she was looking for a girl who was "pure"? "No!", Mrs Armstrong replied strongly. But she agreed she had said Eliza was a good girl: well behaved, that is, and good at cleaning. At one point she described her daughter as a "good little scrubber" with no offence meant or taken by the public gallery.

There could be little doubt when Mrs Armstrong had finished her evidence that she had been at least careless in letting Eliza go with Jarrett, solely on the recommendation of her neighbour Mrs Broughton. But she flatly denied receiving £1 from Jarrett and said she had no money at all from Mrs Broughton. If she had connived in the sale of Eliza, all she got was a shilling from Jarrett. She did not think the clothes bought for Eliza were "smart". She called them "neat". And she had expected to hear from Eliza within a week. Her daughter was a good little scholar and would be able to give an account of how she was getting on.

The evidence of Nancy Broughton did nothing to clarify what had happened in Charles Street when Jarrett had taken Eliza away on 3rd June. In the view of the Secret Commission, Mrs Broughton should have been in the dock rather than appearing as a witness for the prosecution. But she resolutely backed up Mrs Armstrong's account of events, with a few variations, and denied that she knew anything about her friend Becky Jarrett's past life in the vice trade. She had been given a sovereign by her, but that was for past favours when she had cared for Becky during her illness. Nancy and her husband 'Bash' certainly did not run a brothel, as Stead had believed. In its descriptive piece on the Bow Street hearings, the *Pall Mall Gazette* characterised Mrs Broughton as "saucy" but could report no evidence that she was anything other than an out-of-work laundress who liked a drink. Jarrett's claim that she, as well as Mrs Armstrong, were well aware what Eliza was wanted for was vehemently denied.

A good deal was made by the defence lawyers of Mrs Armstrong's willingness to sign the delivery statement Stead had drafted with Mr Thicknesse, the intermediary, when Eliza was handed back to her. Had her daughter not told her about what the French woman had done? Mrs Armstrong said she did not talk to her daughter about that, but she knew anyway from what she had discovered while looking for Eliza. Did she think Eliza looked well when she saw her? Yes, she was taller and she could see she had been well looked after. That was never in dispute. But the issue in court was not whether this thirteen-year-old had had a welcome break from the poverty of her home in Charles Street, as Stead wanted to argue, but whether the so-called Secret Commission had broken the law as charged: taking Eliza from her parents without permission and subjecting her to a physical examination which amounted to indecent assault. There was also the matter of the chloroform. As far as Stead was concerned, that was all irrelevant for when he came to make a speech on his own behalf, he had prepared a lengthy written statement and he imagined the dock at Bow Street would be his pulpit. It was all written out on separate pieces of paper with the idea that he would read each paragraph to the court, then hand a duplicate to the clerk for the record.

The chairman of the Bench, Mr Vaughan, said he had no objections, but reminded Mr Stead that he was not addressing a jury (that would come later if the case was sent to the Old Bailey) and that whatever it was he had to say in his defence must relate to the facts of the case.

"But, your worship," Stead pleaded, "I have been before the country now in this court for five days. The prosecution have urged everything and have called witnesses. I have cross-examined very little, and I presume you will not be hard upon me if I stray somewhat from the strictly technical charge."

Stead still hoped that the Bow Street magistrates would decide not to commit him, and the other accused, to trial by jury at the Central Criminal Court, known as the Old Bailey.

Stead said he had taken legal advice and understood that what he had to say was pertinent to the case. And so he began his soliloquy, trusting that the court would allow him to explain, "fully and frankly as his strength may permit", how it was he had ended up in the dock. Then he went on: "What I did was to expose a conspiracy of vice and crime by a combination ... "

Mr Vaughan interrupted him instantly, saying that this was not permissible evidence. Stead protested that he was charged with conspiracy, when what he had done was expose "a conspiracy of vice and crime". At which Mr Vaughan interjected to say: "Yes, but it has to be done by legal means." Stead said he had used legal means. Mr Vaughan said he had to confine himself to the facts put in evidence. Stead retorted: "Then I am to understand you that it is your worship's ruling that under the English law when I am requested to say why I should not be committed for trial, I am not permitted to make a statement which in concert with my legal advisers I have prepared for my legal defence?"

Mr Vaughan: "I have already told you that you will have every opportunity of commenting, if you choose, upon the facts, and of criticising the law under which you are charged; but I cannot go into the motives which may have induced you to take the course you have done."

Stead: "But, with all due deference to your worship, I understand that the question of motive is in this case the central fact of all". Someone said "Hear, Hear!"

Mr Vaughan: "Motives are immaterial in the charges before me."

Stead would not give up. He unfurled numbered sheets one after the other, each of which was rejected by Vaughan as irrelevant to the case. What they amounted to was an impassioned plea for understanding: if he had broken the law it was for high principle. At one point he told Mr Vaughan that he had considered calling the Archbishop of Canterbury to speak for him. Curtly, Mr Vaughan pointed out that Stead might have thought of it, but he had not done so. Stead managed to blurt out a number of points in defiance of the court ruling. He handed over page No. 9 and began to read:

> "I had no option but to risk all in a desperate attempt to rouse public opinion to a sense of the imperative necessity of forcing through the bill. I made that desperate attempt, I risked all, and I achieved my end."

The increasingly impatient Mr Vaughan said simply: "I cannot receive that."

In the end Stead gave up. What he had wanted to say in court, but was prevented from doing so by Mr Vaughan, was later published by the *Pall Mall Gazette* as "The Suppressed Defence." Stead could not accept that the magistrate was simply sticking to the letter of the law: he regarded him as part of an official conspiracy which had begun with his opponents goading Mrs Armstrong into looking for her daughter and culminated here in a legal gagging. One of the points he wanted to get across was that the Salvation Army was innocent of any misdeeds, even if that meant conceding that he and others had gone further than was strictly permissible.

Part of his published "suppressed evidence" read:

> "I take the earliest opportunity of explaining that the Salvation Army had no part whatever in the operations involving the employment of those subterfuges indispensable for the efficiency of a detective department. They took charge of the girls after I had rescued them—as, for instance, they undertook to train Eliza Armstrong after I had assured them that she had been sold to Rebecca Jarrett for immoral purposes, and that the only hope of rescuing the child from a life of shame was for them to keep her in safety, far away from the vicious surroundings of a drunken home in a Marylebone slum".

Stead ended his lengthy statement with a plea to the Magistrate not to commit him or any of the defendants for trial as there was no case to answer.

> "The case before your worship is not whether any or all of the incidents in the Lily story are true or false, but whether I, and those whom I induced to assist me in this particular transaction are or are not guilty of certain specified offences. I submit that there is no case to submit to a jury for, according to the evidence of witnesses for the prosecution, these offences were never committed. There can be no abduction where there is consent, and the consent of the mother was admittedly given for the departure of the child. Even if she did not, as she says, consent to her going with Jarrett for an immoral purpose, that is beside the question for the child was not taken away for an immoral purpose. If, as they say, she was engaged as a servant, I fulfilled my contract...
>
> The period of the alleged abduction was probably the happiest period in the existence of the child—one

upon which she will look back with regret in the midst of surroundings into which she has been plunged."

He had convinced himself that he had not so much kidnapped Eliza as rescued her from a life of prostitution. Under the subheading: "Who have really injured the Child" he finished his suppressed defence with a flourish:

"I never would have sullied her mind with a whisper of the tale which, in their zeal, our enemies have forced upon her in all its worst suggestiveness. But for the anxiety of some to injure the *Pall Mall Gazette*, and of others to attack the Salvation Army, Eliza Armstrong would, at this moment, have been leading an innocent and industrious life in the midst of happy surroundings, not knowing anything of the fate which enabled us to use her so as to remodel an Act of Parliament, and strengthen the safeguards which the law provides for the protection of the honour and purity of English girls ... If your worship considers that you must commit the case for trial, I beg of you to remember that mine was the guiding brain, and this the directing hand, which alone is responsible for what was done."

All this was to no avail. Stead, and all the others charged with taking and interfering with Eliza, were committed by the Bow Street magistrates for trial by jury at the Old Bailey. Bramwell Booth and Madame Combe were not charged with indecent assault or administering a "noxious" substance. Stead remained indignant that he had not been allowed to preach to the court. Though he had tried hard to avoid a trial at the Old Bailey, he seemed unaware that he had got off lightly: the prosecution at the Old Bailey would examine his journalistic methods much more thoroughly than Mr Vaughan and the bench at Bow Street.

Before the trial began at the Old Bailey, *Lloyd's Weekly* published a letter written to the editor, Thomas Catling, by Mrs Armstrong. It read:

> "Sir, I thank you for the kindness and trouble you have taken in helping restore my child to me; and for the expenses you paid for me to got to Winchester, to make inquiries about my child, and likewise about the woman Jarrett, that took my child away under the pretence that the child was going to a good situation. Instead of that the child was wanted for another purpose, and then set out of the country by the Salvation Army. When they found the mother was determined to have the child back, then they wanted to say that I sold the child, which is all lies. If Mr Bramwell Booth had offered to give me up my child when I applied to him, it would have saved all this bother and trouble. Instead of that he wanted me to pay a hundred pounds. I have lived in the neighbourhood over twenty years, and me and my husband work hard to bring our family up. We bring them up to go to day school and Sunday school. All poor people, when they have a family, are glad when they have left school and are old enough to get a situation. We are glad to let them go to try and do good for themselves, the same as I thought when I let my child go—Your humble servant, Elizabeth Armstrong October 9th".

Stead re-printed the letter in the *Pall Mall Gazette* with the implication that Mrs Armstrong had not acted spontaneously in her efforts to get her daughter back, but had been put up to it by rivals and opponents of his newspaper.

Chapter Thirteen

Revelations at the Old Bailey

It was raining heavily on Friday 23rd October when the Old Bailey trial before Judge Lopes began and the hostile crowds which had barracked the defendants at Bow Street were absent. Everything at the Old Bailey was quieter and more orderly. The *Daily News* noted that Mrs Booth, wife of Bramwell Booth, spent most of her time in court knitting, while Bramwell himself had to call for his ear trumpet so that he could follow proceedings.

At the outset the jury was told by Sir Richard Webster, the Attorney General, who led the prosecution, to disregard whatever it had learned of the case from the newspapers. He explained that one of the charges of abduction had been dropped and that they were proceeding only with a second, and lesser charge, which was classified as a misdemeanor. There were two reasons for this, said Sir Richard Webster. Firstly a newly enacted amendment to the criminal law allowed defendants charged with a misdemeanor to give evidence in court. Secondly, the jury would be free to return home at the end of each day. If the charge had been a felony the jury would have been "locked up" and Stead and the others would have had no chance to explain themselves. Only the French woman, Madame Mourez, was treated differently. She was not charged with abduction but with indecent assault and this was treated, in her case alone, as a felony.

Each of the accused, except Stead, who chose to represent himself, had their advocates. Although the trial at the Old Bailey was to a large extent a repeat of that at Bow Street, rigorous cross examination of both the defendants and witnesses brought many revelations. In particular, Stead, the central figure in the drama, was exposed as a man whose self-righteousness appeared to blind him to the callousness of his actions. His approach to journalism proved to be, at best, shoddy, and at worst, downright dishonest. In further cross examination of the witnesses, and of Stead himself, many more of the details of the £5 virgin saga were revealed.

At the Old Bailey, Eliza spoke of her first interview with Stead. She told the court:

> "Mr Stead asked me if I went to school, and I said "Yes". He asked me where and I said "a Board School". He asked me if I went to Sunday school. I said "Yes". What did you tell him? That I went to Harrow-road Sunday school at nine o'clock in the morning and in the afternoon too. I also said that I went to the District Sunday School on Sunday nights. That was true? Yes. I had attended those schools for four years. He asked me if there were any treats there, and I said I had been once to Epping Forest and once to Richmond."

Stead was forced to admit how he had come by the touching little verse attributed to 'Lily' in his Maiden Tribute investigation. He took it from the letter Eliza had written to her mother from Paris and which had been given to Bramwell Booth. Cross examined Stead said:

> "I read it through, and I had considerable doubt about what to do about the matter—from one point of view it would have been very good to have sent it to the mother, but from what seemed to me the chief point of view, that the mother should not get the child again to sell her to vice, I thought it was better to suppress the letter, and I suppressed the letter accordingly, and it is here…"

He still had the letter. Eliza had written her Paris address on it but someone had made it illegible. Stead said he did not know who had done this but he said his impression was that

> "the address was a right address at first, and was subsequently altered in order to avoid giving the

111

mother a clue to where her child was, so that she might regain the child, that she only wanted to get her in order to sell her to vice again."

Stead admitted at the Old Bailey that he knew on 11th July that Mrs Armstrong had applied to the magistrate, Mr Cooke, in Marylebone to help find her daughter:

"I saw that Mrs Armstrong had appeared before Mr Cooke, and that he had scolded her, and had said she was a very negligent woman, and so on."

His reason for ignoring her appeal was that the police did not get in touch with him. Stead wanted to contend that if there had been a serious attempt to find out where Eliza was, and it was assumed she was the girl 'Lily', then someone should have put the question to him, editor of the *Pall Mall Gazette*. But nobody ever did.

He interrogated Inspector Edward Borner, the police officer principally charged with finding Eliza, about why he had not applied to the *Gazette* for information. Quite reasonably, Borner replied that he had simply been asked to find a missing girl, not to discover who the girl 'Lily' was in the *Gazette*'s investigation. In fact it was some time before he knew of the similarities between Stead's description of 'Lily' and Eliza Armstrong.

Borner's line of investigation began when he read the letters that had been sent from the woman called Mrs Sullivan to her friend Mrs Broughton. These had led him to Hope Cottage in Winchester and to the Salvation Army. Once he was satisfied that it was this organisation which had Eliza in its care, his job was to see that she was returned to her mother. This was achieved by questioning Mr Bramwell Booth as to Eliza's whereabouts. As far as Borner was concerned Stead was neither a help nor a hindrance in his quest to find Eliza. And in his pursuit of the person who had taken Eliza from her mother, Borner felt he need look no further than Rebecca Jarrett, who had been easy enough to identify despite her adopted name of Mrs Sullivan.

All the while, until his sudden confession at St James's Hall on 21st August that he had been responsible for the disappearance of Eliza, Stead had remained silent. It was only when he was questioned closely at the Old Bailey that it became clear how devious he had been, and how anxious he was that what had really happened to Eliza should not be made public. He had had an opportunity to speak to Mrs Armstrong when she had made a surprise appearance at one of the hearings of the Mansion House Committee that Stead had set up to "verify" the facts of the Maiden Tribute articles. Stead had watched Mrs Armstrong as she pleaded for information on Eliza's whereabouts and what had happened to her. At the Old Bailey he was asked what he had made of the first occasion on which he had set eyes on the drunken mother he believed had sold her daughter to a brothel. Stead told the Old Bailey:

> "Mr Thomas brought Mrs Armstrong down—she was lying under the shadow of a great charge—it was obviously in her interest, I thought, to try to disprove the charge–she goes to the police court in order to clear her character from that charge—she goes to the Mansion House and there says various things, which to my mind did not leave an impression that she wanted her child back."

He agreed, however, that Mrs Armstrong had said quite clearly "I want my child" and that she had burst out crying before the Mansion House Committee. Stead was not sure how to interpret this behaviour and told the jury at the Old Bailey:

> "… you have seen people of this kind crying, and their crying does not prove the sincerity of their feelings; there is a kind of drunken crying—she was not drunk, but she had that kind of maudlin way, and

my impression was the same as Cardinal Manning's, and I talked to him about it, and I did not think that at the Mansion House she formulated a demand 'I really want my child back'—I thought she was more anxious to know who had taken her away, and whether her child was quite safe, than anything else; and two days afterwards the police, who were in constant communication with the woman, said that she would be satisfied with an assurance that the child was well, and would let her stop; then I thought it was all nonsense: I thought Mr Thomas had put her up to it."

The only time Stead had seen Mrs Armstrong before he appeared at Bow Street was at the Mansion House. He conceded in court that everything he thought he knew about her and the circumstances of Eliza's going away he had got from Jarrett. At no time had he thought to verify anything Jarrett had told him. He had never been to Charles Street, though he had sent some people there on his behalf to find out what kind of a place it was. He accepted that Nancy Broughton, Mrs Jarrett's friend did not run a brothel, but he still thought she was a procuress. In fact, he thought Eliza was bought from Broughton rather than from the mother directly.

Not only had Stead not bothered to verify any of the circumstances of Eliza's purchase, relying entirely on what Jarrett told him, he could not be sure he had remembered what she had said all that well. Cross examined, he told the court:

"Altogether between 24th May and the 3rd June I saw Jarrett to have a conversation with her about three or four times, four or five times that might be—in those conversations several young girls were spoken of, said to be in several distinct places—I don't think I ever committed to writing in any definite form what purported to be Mrs Jarrett's statement to me... I have just handed in the narrative as I wrote it for the first time, as near as I can remember, on the 28th or 29th of June—that contains the story—the first part of it, relating to the purchase, is, as near as I can remember, what Jarrett told me on the night of 3rd June—"

"I did not write it down until three or four weeks after, during which time I had been through a Ministerial crisis, which in itself was rather exciting... the government changed hands, and Mr Gladstone went out and Lord Salisbury came in—that naturally increased the strain and tension upon me during the time of the crisis—before and subsequently I was in the habit at nights of going to brothels to meet brothel-keepers as a customer, and to drink with brothel-keepers—I am a teetotaler—it was difficult for me to drink champagne, and therefore I would say in justice to Jarrett, that drinking and smoking as I was not used to it before I undertook the inquiry, I might have confused some of the details of what Jarrett told me... I have told the story as near as possible as it was told to me as I remembered it—but I took no notes at the time..."

Asked why he had changed the name Eliza to Lily in his story he said it was partly to "protect" Mrs Armstrong and Mrs Broughton and partly because he had "compounded two stories" one of Eliza and the other of another girl who was "actually outraged". Stead offered to bring the other girl to the witness box; Judge Lopes thought it was unnecessary.

Listening to Stead's account of how he came to judge the Armstrong's as a family though he had met only Eliza, the foreman of the jury inquired if he had not thought to ask her about her mother and father.

"I don't think I ever asked the child about her parents..." Stead began. "I thought they were drunken parents, and that the mother had sold her into vice, and I did not want to ask her—if I could have seen before as well as I see behind, it would have been wiser to have asked her if they were kind parents, but it never crossed my mind—I have no doubt now what her answer would have been, yes as to the mother, I do not know anything about the father (ie the man he had described in the *Gazette* as a drunkard), but I also relied on Mrs Butler's statement that Jarrett was an entirely reformed woman—it would have been discreet to have asked the child about the parents if I had known what I know now—she appeared to be a cheerful and truthful child... I knew nothing of her education until I got that letter which has been put in—the child herself told me about going to Epping and Richmond —I asked her because I wanted to know how much she had seen of the world—I wished to know whether she had lived in a slum all her life."

Now and again, as he was quizzed about the impression Eliza had made on him, Stead lost his composure. At one point the Attorney General, Sir Richard Webster asked him:

"When the little child came to you and told you of her child-life, and that she had been sent to Sunday-schools, and was regularly attending Sunday schools..."

Stead interrupted Webster:

"She did not say 'regularly': I still thought she was in the market, why should I not? There are plenty of mothers whose children go to Sunday-schools who perfectly ready to assent to their seduction, just as there are rich mothers who sell them to rich husbands who do not love them a bit; I think it is just as immoral in the one case as in the other."

Contradicting his own evidence in which he made it clear that he wanted to do everything he could to prevent Eliza returning to her mother, he exclaimed:

> "I say that I always gave the assurance that I would give the child up if the mother wished her back, if her mother really wished her back—I thought she would be used as a catspaw by those who had a spite against the Salvation Army and a spite against the *Pall Mall Gazette*…"

At the Old Bailey Stead stuck doggedly to the notion that Mrs Armstrong, a woman he knew nothing about, could not possibly have any affection for her daughter. Not only that, it became clear that he had reneged on an agreement he had both with Rebecca Jarrett and Mrs Josephine Butler that any girls acquired in the course of the Maiden Tribute investigation would be handed over to them. As Stead was defending himself, and was able to examine those in the dock, in time he came to question Rebecca Jarrett herself. There were some heated exchanges.

Jarrett insisted that Stead had muddled up the stories she had told him about her efforts to find him a 13-year-old girl. Stead began to suggest that Jarrett was perhaps an unreliable witness and that she had not told him the whole truth. This was a dangerous course to take for he had admitted that his account in the Maiden Tribute of the buying of the girl 'Lily' was based entirely on what Jarrett had told him. Jarrett stuck to her story that Mrs Armstrong had allowed Eliza to go on the understanding that it was "for a gentleman", in other words, for immoral purposes. Eliza's father, however, was not a party to this agreement; Jarrett had not met him and knew nothing about him. Stead's description of Charles Armstrong as a drunkard who did not care what happened to his daughter was pure invention, a piece of fiction with which he sought to embroider the Maiden Tribute melodrama.

Stead was unaware that Jarrett had told Mrs Armstrong that Eliza could write to her, perhaps once month. This was clearly contrary to Stead's plans for the girl as he intended to sever all connections with Charles Street which he believed was, as he put it at the St James's Hall meeting, "steeped in vice." Jarrett herself found it hard to explain in court why she had wanted to ensure Eliza kept in touch with her mother and why she had written letters to Nancy Broughton assuring her Eliza was in her care living in Winchester.

The Old Bailey transcript of Stead's questioning of Jarrett has the following:

> "I knew no harm was going to be done to the little child, but the mother did not know that—I knew that after I took the child away the mother would remember that she had let the child go to be ruined; I wanted to spare the mother that feeling, if possible—I said once that she should write now and then to her mother—I did not tell you (Stead) that—I believe I said to you ' What are you going to do with her?'—you answered that you were going to send her away for a little while, and then I should have her—I wanted her very much, and I always wanted the child sent to me at Winchester, whatever child I bought, and you promised that I should have that child sent to me... in order that I might bring it up—I told Mrs Butler that one chief reason why I wanted the child at Winchester was that I might be able to take it back safe and sound to its mother, in order to show the mother that I had done it no harm... to the best of my belief from what I told you, you believed the girl belonged to you—I was very uneasy about her stopping in Paris so long—I thought I was rather badly treated by you—I thought you ought to let me have the child back, because you promised me."

In the short time Eliza had known Jarrett she had become attached to her. It had never been Stead's intention for Jarrett to accompany Eliza when she was sent to Paris but Eliza refused to go without her. Jarrett returned after a few days and went back to Hope Cottage to continue as the matron working for Josephine Butler who had introduced her to Stead. When Rebecca had stepped down from the witness box, the initial link between her and Stead, Josephine Butler, made a brief appearance. It was she who had vouched for Rebecca's honesty and the fact that she was a reformed woman.

Stead cross-examined Mrs Butler, recalling the discussions they had had about rescuing vulnerable you girls. She said, she, Stead and Bramwell Booth had all agreed that

> "we had only to buy girls that were in the market, and that would otherwise in all probability be ruined—I entirely understood that and I brought forward by analogy from the abolitionists in America appearing in the slave market and buying young girls who would otherwise have been sold into slavery, in order to set them free—it was on that understanding that I consented to Jarrett being employed by you; and I undertook to provide a home for any number of young girls she might purchase; and I would have taken Eliza Armstrong most gladly if she had been sent to me."

Mrs Butler said she had arranged for Eliza to be sent to her from Paris, but for some reason she did not turn up.

Before Stead took the stand at the Old Bailey, there were already cracks appearing in the armoury of the Secret Commission. He began with a matter of fact account of how he had come to take up the cause of the Criminal Law Amendment Act, prompted at first by a plea from Benjamin Scott, Chamberlain of the City of London who had put together a commission to investigate the 'white slave trade'. He described his first meeting with Rebecca Jarrett in which she had told him about the procuring of innocent young girls giving him a number of details 'of a most ghastly character'. When she was reluctant to get involved with plying her old trade on his behalf he had remonstrated with her saying

> "she deserved, if what she said was true, to be hanged in this world and damned in the next, and the least she could do was to make what reparation she could for crimes which she had confessed—I think that argument had weight with her."

Without any of the histrionics that had upset the magistrate at Bow Street, Stead ran through the whole sequence of events from the time he met Eliza to her delivery to the French 'abortionist', to the Poland Street brothel. There was at the Old Bailey a revelation which had not emerged at Bow Street and Stead had hoped would remain unreported. When he had got Jarrett and Eliza out of Poland Street, he dismissed Jacques for the night as his job was done, and went in search of Bramwell Booth. He was in a panic because he had entered the room where the girl had been put to bed in the brothel and he feared he might be accused of violating her. He asked Booth if he could find a physician in the early hours of the morning who would agree, for a fee, to come out and examine her and to provide a certificate to say she was still a virgin after the visit to Poland Street.

Dr Heywood Smith, a gynaecologist at the British Lying-in Hospital in Endell Street, Bloomsbury and a Member of the Royal College of Physicians, was called from his bed to perform this very unusual examination. Stead recognised now that what he had asked the doctor to do was quite unethical and he sat on the certificate Heywood Smith had signed in order to 'keep him out of trouble.' But Borner did not give up and Heywood Smith appeared at the Old Bailey on subpoena, a deeply embarrassing occasion for him.

The story he had to tell was quite shocking. On the night of the 3rd June he had been called upon by Stead at his home in Harley Street. With Stead were Jarrett (who was still calling herself Mrs Sullivan) and the girl he now knew was Eliza Armstrong. He had been introduced to Stead some months earlier by Bramwell Booth whom he knew well, though he was not himself a member of the Salvation Army. While Jarrett and Eliza waited outside Stead explained to Heywood Smith that the girl was to be taken in by the Salvation Army and before he handed her over he wanted to be sure she was not a prostitute. This was Heywood Smith's version of the conversation anyway. Stead told him about the French woman Madame Mourez and her examination. After a while Heywood Smith agreed to examine Eliza. He would not do so in his own home but instead sent a note to a woman called Sarah Hutchinson who had rooms at 27 Nottingham Place and sometimes took in his patients if they had to stay near Harley Street for days at a time.

Miss Hutchinson was also called to the Old Bailey. She told the court:

> "I had gone to bed in the usual course, and late at night, or rather early next morning, I was aroused by the ringing of the night bell—I think it was between 12 o'clock and 1 o'clock... I went on the landing and heard the doctor's son, whose house it is, speak—I then heard that the persons at the door wanted to see me and went down and saw Mr Stead—I had never seen him before that—and he said he had brought a note from Dr Heywood Smith and gave it to me: 'Can you take in Mrs Sullivan and the child who accompanies her–an urgent case? We will call in two hours. Money no object'."

She asked Stead if it would be a long case as she only had one room left, but he said he thought not.

Stead went away leaving Miss Hutchinson to look after Jarrett and Eliza. She made up beds for them and when they had settled down she sat up waiting for Dr Heywood Smith. He arrived at about three o'clock in the morning.

The doctor picked up some chloroform that Miss Hutchinson kept in her living room and told her to go and wake up Jarrett but to keep the child asleep if possible. Jarrett stayed in bed awake while Miss Hutchinson, complying with the doctor's orders, began to put a handkerchief soaked in chloroform over Eliza's mouth. Dr Heywood Smith then continued to administer the chloroform himself and after some minutes asked Miss Hutchinson if she had any Vaseline. She went upstairs to find some for him. Then she left the room and could say no more about what happened.

In his evidence Dr Heywood Smith said that he examined Eliza in the presence of Jarrett. It was simply a matter of inserting a finger. For this he charged three guineas which Mr Stead paid later by cheque. Miss Hutchinson received a guinea for taking in Jarrett and Eliza. The certificate was intended for Stead but for some reason was sent first to Bramwell Booth. It read simply:

"18 Harley Street, Cavendish Square, June 4th 1885

I herby certify that I have this day examined Eliza Armstrong, and have found her virgo intacta, and I am convinced that no one has ever attempted criminal intercourse with her. Heywood Smith M.D. Physician to the Hospital for Women and British Lying-in Hospital."

Although Dr Heywood Smith had committed at Stead's behest exactly the same indecent assault on Eliza as Madame Mourez he was not charged with any offence. He clearly understood that what he did was out of the ordinary—in fact, he had never had a case like it before—and attempted to justify his examination by saying he was convinced the child was "bought." Here again, that slave analogy came to mind. Because the child was purchased Stead could do what he like with her. He had not freed her from slavery, he had enslaved her. Clearly in Stead's mind this was of great significance. If Jarrett had simply gone about her old profession in her accustomed fashion and taken a girl on the pretence of offering her work as a servant then that girl would have been acquired by deception and would not then have been 'purchased on the open market.' She would not therefore be the property of Stead or his accomplice Mrs Butler or of the Salvation Army.

As he was too busy himself to arrange the reunion of Eliza and her mother, he sent Mr Jacques with instructions "to endeavour to save Eliza Armstrong from the pollution of going back to Charles Street, and hearing the whole question discussed about the Lily story, and that the best thing would be to offer her another situation where her mother could see her and see that all was right."

The truth about Stead's creation of the story he wrote up as "A girl of thirteen bought for £5" emerged in bits and pieces. He was obliged to produce the hand written drafts all of which referred specifically to "Eliza" and to no other girls. As a last ditch attempt to convince the court that the story of 'Lily' was an amalgam of Eliza's experience and another girl's he offered, at the last minute, to bring the other violated girl to court. The judge dismissed this offer as irrelevant. And Stead's desperate attempt to convince the jury that he knew of a girl who had been violated in the very Poland Street brothel where Eliza had been taken was not helped by his admission that it was not he who had chosen that house of ill-fame for the mock-rape, but Sampson Jacques. He knew nothing about Poland Street before his brief visit there on the night of 3rd June.

As the proceedings dragged on, Stead realised that the game was up. He once again asked the court permission to call the Archbishop of Canterbury and other moral dignitaries to speak to his fine motives, but Judge Lopes waved this aside. When he was not giving evidence or cross examining himself or other witnesses, Stead sat scribbling notes and letters. One note he wrote has been preserved and gives some idea of his state of mind. It was addressed to an old friend and fellow campaigner Mrs Millicent Fawcett:

> "Private
> The Dock Old Bailey
> November 7 1885
> Dear Mrs Fawcett
>
> Will you pardon me who is all but a convicted criminal to say just one word of heartfelt gratitude and more, to you who have been so good and kind to me who has made such a mess of things is now going to gaol with a feeling of satisfaction born of a hope that my imprisonment may be some atonement for all my blunders and all the trouble I have brought upon so many good people.
>
> God bless you and keep you from ever again having to defend so poor a creature as,
>
> Yours in sincere humiliation, William T. Stead."

Stead was in trouble with his friends, especially the Salvation Army which was acutely embarrassed that their Chief of Staff Bramwell Booth and another uniformed member, Mrs Combe were in the dock at the Old Bailey. The Army's founder, William Booth, believed that Stead had misled Bramwell. Stead's account of how Eliza had been "purchased" was much more clear cut than the evidence allowed. The jury at the Old Bailey was coming to the same conclusion. And they were concerned to know how Stead had arrived at the very low opinion he had of the Armstrong family, the mother in particular.

POLICE NEWS

LAW COURTS AND WEEKLY RECORD.

No. 1,126. SATURDAY, SEPTEMBER 12, 1885. Price One Penny.

Chapter Fourteen
The judge and the jury

Much of the evidence in court had to do with the comings and goings in Charles Street on the 2nd and 3rd of June and the question of whether or not Mrs Armstrong had any idea Eliza was being taken for "immoral purposes". It was therefore something of a surprise when, in his summing up, Judge Lopes said it was sufficient for the jury to decide whether or not Eliza had been taken without the permission of her father. Why the prosecution case was reduced to this is not clear, for the charges of abduction clearly stated that they referred to the taking of Eliza from "the mother and the father". It is likely the judge thought it would help if the jury did not have to come to a judgement on whether or not Mrs Armstrong sold Eliza, because even if she had done so, and it was without Charles Armstrong's consent, Stead and his accomplices would still have been guilty. In evidence, Charles Armstrong had said that when he first asked his wife where Eliza had gone, she said she thought it was Croydon. That was not bad, he thought, because he could "borrow his brother-in-law's pony and trap and get there in a couple of hours" to see her. It was when his wife admitted that she did not know the address, nor the name of the woman who had taken Eliza, that he lost his temper and struck her.

Rebecca could not say if Eliza's father knew she was going, and though Stead had implied in the Maiden Tribute story that Mr Armstrong was a drunk and would not care, he had no evidence for this. So the case was open and shut: Eliza was taken without her father's permission and therefore those in the dock were guilty. The only question the jury could debate was whether or not they were all equally guilty. What about Bramwell Booth and Mrs Combe? They had acted in good faith on the story told to them by Stead, that Eliza had been sold for immoral purposes. Booth was, tangentially, involved in the alleged transaction because he had agreed to look after any girls procured for Stead. Mrs Combe, on the other hand, was called in at the last minute to care for Eliza and had nothing to do with her abduction in the first place. Mr Sampson Jacques, who kept a very low profile throughout, was merely a hired hand and was not directly involved in taking Eliza from Charles Street.

The jury had difficulty in coming to a decision about Stead's culpability and returned after they had retired to ask Judge Lopes for guidance:

> "Our difficulty is this," said the foreman. "that if Jarrett obtained the child by false pretences, we feel it was directly contrary to Stead's intentions. We find it, therefore, difficult as businessmen to hold him criminally responsible for that which, if he had known it, he would have repudiated."

Judge Lopes dismissed that problem as irrelevant. After three hours the jury delivered its verdict. Stead and Jarrett were found guilty. Booth and Jacques were acquitted, and the case against Mdme Combe had been dropped earlier in the trial. The Salvation Army had escaped conviction, but Mr Jacques was not free to go. He, along with Madame Mourez, Stead and Jarrett were all charged with indecently assaulting Eliza at Milton Street. No sentences were passed on the first count of abduction until a second hearing before a different jury on the charge of indecent assault. Judge Lopes had dismissed the first jury on the grounds that they had had enough to deal with deciding the abduction case.

On 10th November, in the Old Court at the Bailey, there was a brief re-run of the evidence relating to Eliza's examination by Madame Mourez at Milton Street on the night of 3rd June. The cab driver who had taken Jarrett and Eliza from Madame Mourez to Poland Street gave his story, much as he had given it to *Lloyd's Weekly* in the summer. He was on the rank at Great Quebec Street around 9.30 pm when a man he could now identify as Mr Jacques, asked him to pull up near to, but not outside, 3 Milton Street. When he got there another man, he now knew to be Mr Stead, spoke to him. After a brief discussion he was told to go to Poland Street, taking Jarrett and Eliza. When he got there, Jarrett got out to get some change at the ham and beef shop. He noticed then to two men from Milton Street in the road; they must have followed immediately. Mr Smith got his fare and drove away. In evidence at Bow Street he had spoken of his suspicion about what these men were up to.

Eliza told what had happened to her, once again, and was questioned briefly by Jarrett and Jacques. She said she did not "cry out" or complain when Madame Mourez examined her because she was frightened. She did not tell anybody what had happened. But none of that was relevant. There was really no dispute that Stead with the help of Jacques and Jarrett had arranged for Madame Mourez to make a physical examination of Eliza's vagina for which there was no justification, legal or otherwise.

Judge Lopes handed down the sentences. Stead got three months, Jarrett six months and Jacques one month, all "without hard labour", a concession perhaps to Stead's social status and the 'motives' of those involved. It was Madame Mourez, who spoke little English and did not understand much of what was said in court, who came off worst. She got six months hard labour though she was in her seventies.

Finally, the judge, while acknowledging that Stead had made a most moving and effective speech on his own behalf, gave his opinion on the abduction of Eliza:

> "The result is that your experiment, instead of proving what it was intended to prove, has absolutely and entirely failed, for the jury have found that Eliza

Armstrong, the subject of that experiment, was never bought for immoral purposes at all. I regret to say that you thought fit to publish in the *Pall Mall Gazette* a distorted account of the case of Eliza Armstrong, and that you deluged, some months ago, our streets and the whole country with an amount of filth which has, as I fear, tainted the minds of the children that you were so anxious to protect, and which has been—and I don't hesitate to say, ever will be—a disgrace to journalism. An irreparable injury has been done to the parents of this child, and they have been subjected to the unutterable scandal and ignominy of having sold their child for violation. The child has been dragged through the dirt, examined by a woman who bears, or, in your opinion, at any rate, bore a foul character, subjected to chloroform, taken to a brothel, and then sent to the South of France, her letters to her mother suppressed, and the child refused when demanded. All that has been done by you, relying on the statements of a woman whose character you knew and whom you trusted with money—and I think this no small part of the offence you committed—to bribe parents to commit the greatest sin they could commit—viz. to sell their own children for immoral purposes."

Nevertheless, when they delivered their verdict on the abduction charge, the jury gave a nod in Stead's direction, in a statement which urged the government to ensure efficient administration of the Criminal Law Amendment Act for the protection of children. Judge Lopes took note and handed out a sentence which he said was far more lenient than it would have been had Stead taken Eliza for "immoral purposes". He need not have been so understanding, for the prisoner led down to the cells and taken to Newgate prison was in a kind of ecstasy of martyrdom as he said goodbye to his wife and friends.

Jail, it turned out, was almost too good for him.

PRISON LIFE OF STEAD
STEAD PICKING OAKUM
STEAD EATING HIS SKILLY
THE ARMSTRONG ABDUCTION CASE – STEAD IN PRISON
R
2-8.
STEAD IN PRISON
ARRIVAL AT COLDBATH FIELDS
MR STEAD AND HIS VISITOR

Chapter Fifteen
The joy of prison

Like a good Christian, Stead forgave his persecutors and settled down to a few pleasant weeks behind bars. His sentence—which was for the two charges on which he was convicted—was to run from the time of the indictment and there was therefore just over two months left to serve, though it did mean that he would spend Christmas in jail. Stead wrote up his experience in a pamphlet 'My first imprisonment'.

He described how he and Jacques were first taken into the cells of Newgate Prison which adjoined the Court House (the present Old Bailey was built on the site of the prison). It was almost empty which "added the chill and silence of the grave." It had a feel of stone and iron, hard and cold as a turn-key led them through one clanking gate to another. Even there Stead felt a weight off his shoulders:

> "At last, after years of incessant stress and strain, and after six months in which every hour had to get through the work of two, I had come to a place where time was a drug in the market—where time was to hang heavily on my hands, after being long bankrupt in minutes, I was to be a millionaire of hours."

A horse-drawn prison van took them from there to Coldbath-in-the-Fields and as it left Newgate they could hear

> "the hoarse roar of the crowd which had waited to give us a parting yell of execration as we left the scene in which for so many days we had been the central figures. It was a poor howl, the crowd apparently being small, but like Don Silva in the Spanish Gypsy, when Father Isidor was hanged we:
> Knew the shout
> For wonted exultation of the crowd

When malefactors die—or saints or heroes.
It was the last sound from the outside world we heard."

At Coldbath they got their prison uniforms and began to mingle with the regular run of London villains. Stead reported that one asked him: "Do you know how much them wot was in the Armstrong case has got?" When Stead told him who he was, and his sentence, the response was: "You've got off cheap."

This first night he had no special privileges: he was given a bath, which was clean but chilly, his own clothes were taken and he was given breeches of "a most lovely hue—a fine shade of rich creamy-coloured yellow, plentifully bespattered with broad arrow." It took some time to find prison clothes large enough to fit the portly Jacques. The gruel they were given Stead could not swallow and he thought with longing of the waiter at the London club where he had dined the night before. He said goodbye to the badly wrapped Jacques and was shown his cell, which was simple but "not a bad kind of retreat, immeasurably superior to all the hermit's cells I had seen or heard of."

Stead was allowed no mattress on his plank bed at Coldbath Fields. He had a table and chair, a gas jet for lighting. In the morning, after a fitful night, he was put to picking oakum, a standard task in prisons, workhouses and asylums. This was old hemp rope from ships that was unpicked, and then re-twisted roughly and covered in tar to be used in calking: it was, as in the saying, "money for old rope". Stead wrote:

> "It was not proper oakum but coir fibre. I had to pick from ten ounces to one pound. It is an excellent meditative occupation. But it is hard on the finger nails. Mine wanted trimming; for if the nails are not short, the leverage on the nail in disentangling the fibre causes considerable suffering. 'How do prisoners do

when they want their nails cut?' I asked. 'Bite'em' laconically replied the warder."

Stead lived the harsh prison life at Coldbath-in-the-Fields for just three days, during which time he had a number of visitors, the last of whom brought him the welcome news that the Home Secretary had classified him as a 'first class misdemeanant' after entreaties from his influential friends, notably Lord Shaftsbury. He handed back his prison clothes and within an hour was in a handsome cab on his way to a life of luxury in Holloway Prison, a fairy castle of a building which at the time took in more male than female prisoners.

Of his time in Holloway, when he even had his own servant, Stead wrote:

"At a quarter to six I rose and made my bed, and dressed, then shook and rolled up the hearthrugs and matting, and set to work. At half past six the surety—a poor fellow who is in for six months because he cannot find two sureties for £25 to answer for his abstention from threats— 'I was forsworn,' he said to me,'and my brother-in-law said I would be forsworn again'—came in, lit the fire, washed up the crockery, and generally put things to rights...

Never had I a pleasanter holiday, a more charming season of repose... I had sought it in vain in Switzerland (he had been at the resort of Grindelwald when the warrant was issued for his arrest) but I found it in Holloway. Here, as in an enchanted castle, jealously guarded by liveried retainers, I was kept secure from the strife of tongues, and afforded the rare luxury of journalistic leisure. From the governor, Colonel Milman, to the poor fellow who scrubbed out my room, everyone was as kind as kind could be. From all parts of the Empire, even from distant Fiji, rained down upon me every morning the benedictions of men and women who had felt in the midst of their life-long labours for the outcast the unexpected life of the great outburst of compassion and indignation which followed publication of the 'Maiden Tribute'. I had the papers, books, letters, flowers, everything that heart could wish.

Twice a week my wife brought the sunlight of her presence into the pretty room, all hung around with Christmas greetings from absent friends, and twice a week she brought with her one of the children. On the day after Christmas the whole family came, excepting the little two-year-old, and what high jinks we had in the old goal with all the bairns! The room was rather small for blind man's buff, but we managed it somehow, and never was there a merrier little party than that which met in cell No. 2 on the ground floor of E wing of Holloway Gaol..."

Before his "blazing" fire, Stead was able to receive comic gifts from the *Gazette* staff, including a muzzled imitation

Stead's sketch of his luxurious cell in Holloway Prison.
A servant cleaned his room and lit the fire.

dog which barked. His tears flowed when the prisoners sang together the carol Hark the Herald Angels, and he had his maudlin moments. He even, on occasion, expressed regret about what had happened to Rebecca Jarrett. And to Dr Heywood Smith, so horribly embarrassed at the Old Bailey. But not a word about the Armstrongs or little Eliza. No concern about how she was "gittin on" even though the long arm of the law had reached out and taken her back to a place Stead believed was "steeped in sin."

In his prison diary, Stead wrote:

"I know of no one who ever loved me who does not love me still. I know of no one who was a friend who has turned out a foe. Some acquaintances, perhaps two or three, have been somewhat queer, but I cannot say that I have a personal enemy in the world. I don't feel like an enemy to any one. I am all compassed about and borne up and inspired with a love which is marvellous."

However, despite the state of grace in which he wallowed in Holloway, Stead had not quite given up on putting the record straight about Eliza Armstrong.

Chapter Sixteen
Still lying about Eliza

In November 1910, the Editor of the *Penny Illustrated Paper* asked Stead if he would give an account of why, twenty five years earlier, he had been sent to jail. Stead duly obliged with yet another bowdlerised version of events. He wrote:

> "All that the enemy could hope to secure by way of consolation was a verdict against the defendants for failing to produce evidence to prove the consent of the parents to the abduction of their daughter. It was admitted that the child had never been better cared for in her life. It was proved that the only reason she had not been returned to her mother, was the belief, which the police shared, that if she went back she would be sold in deadly earnest next time."

In all the thousands of words of evidence recorded in the newspaper reports of the Bow Street hearings and the Old Bailey trial there is not one suggestion by Inspector Borner, nor by any other police officer, that Eliza was in danger of being sold into prostitution if she were returned to her mother and father. Nor is there any comment by the police that she was better off as a captive servant than she was at home. There was one exchange between Bramwell Booth and Inspector Borner at the Salvation Army headquarters which might have been construed as such. Booth asked Borner if Eliza might not be better off where she was in France than back in Charles Street. Borner, uncharacteristically, gave nodding agreement. But there is no hint that he thought that Eliza would be "back on the open market" to be sold to a brothel.

Stead followed this calumny with:

> "But the consent of the father had never been obtained, and the judge ruled that this was fatal to our

defence and that the jury had no option but to return a verdict of guilty. But if I had persisted in asking one question, this fatal fault would have been wiped out. I wanted to ask the mother for her marriage lines. Sir Charles Russell, who was leading counsel on our side (he represented Jarrett but not Stead) protested against a question that imputed immorality to any woman, no matter how degraded she might be, unless there was solid basis to go upon. I said that I had nothing to go upon beyond the fact that she was admittedly a drunken woman, who in my belief had sold her own daughter into prostitution.' 'That' said the great barrister, 'is not enough. I will never be party to such licence of cross-examination.'

What a let-off for Mrs Armstrong, Stead implied. He continued:

"I gladly concurred, for I had frequently protested against the way in which women were insulted in the witness-box by cross-examining counsel. But months after I had been in gaol, it was discovered at Somerset House that the child had been born out of wedlock, and that the nominal father had no legal rights over the girl who bore his name. It was then too late, and I have never ceased to be grateful that the fact was not discovered till afterwards. If I had asked the question I should probably have been acquitted and so have lost that experience in prison which was one of the most valuable lessons of my life..."

There is nothing on Eliza Armstrong's birth certificate to indicate that she is not legitimate, nor that Charles Armstrong was not her legal father. She had been born on 18 April 1872 at the family home which was then 9 Charles Street, Lisson Grove. Her father is given as Charles Armstrong, a sweep, and her mother Elizabeth Armstrong (formerly Chivers). This does not prove, however, that the parents were married at the time of

Eliza's birth. Whoever Stead got to delve into the archives at Somerset House had gone further and searched for the Armstrong's marriage certificate. This reveals that they did not marry until two years after Eliza was born, in March 1874. So it was true that Charles Armstrong was not the legal father of Eliza. Whether or not that would be been fatal for the abduction charge is far from clear, however. On the one hand, if the court had known this, it is very unlikely Judge Lopes would have simplified the case for the jury in the way he did, putting all the emphasis on the taking away without consent from the father. The original abduction charge included the taking of Eliza from her mother.

And Stead was not convicted only on the charge of abduction. He was found guilty of indecent assault on Eliza. Her legitimacy had no bearing on this crime which was possibly far more serious in the judge's view than the abduction. And he was spared a further charge of indecent assault when the decision was taken not to prosecute Dr Heywood Smith. Stead consistently omitted these offences in all the accounts he gave of his trial between his release from Holloway and his death in 1912. He had a reputation as an affectionate family man who loved children. He wrote books for "little bairns". And yet, though he judged Eliza to be a good, innocent girl, he arranged for her to be indecently assaulted twice. It is surely inconceivable Stead would have subjected his own daughters to a vaginal examination. He never apologised to Eliza or to her parents for this gross and quite unjustified assault. He remained, until his death, resolutely righteous and seemingly oblivious to his appalling behaviour. In 'Why I was sent to Prison' he wrote:

> "Looking back over the whole episode, I can only say now, as I said then, that when I die, I wish for no other epitaph upon my tomb than this:

Here lies the man who wrote
The Maiden Tribute of Modern Babylon."

Though Stead's body was never recovered from the Atlantic there are monuments to his memory in both New York and London and the epitaph he wished for is chiseled in stone in the graveyard in which his parents were buried in North Shields, on Tyneside. It was where his father had been a Congregationalist minister and Stead spent most of his childhood. Several family members are buried here in Preston cemetery. Stead's epitaph reads:

ALSO OF THEIR SON WILLIAM THOMAS STEAD
JOURNALIST
CHAMPION OF DEFENCELESS WOMANHOOD
APOSTLE OF UNIVERSAL PEACE
FOUNDER OF THE "REVIEW OF REVIEWS"
AND AUTHOR OF
"THE MAIDEN TRIBUTE OF MODERN BABYLON" (1885)
WHO WENT DOWN WITH THE "TITANIC"
IN MID-ATLANTIC
APRIL 15TH 1912, AGED 62 YEARS

Chapter Seventeen
The aftermath

Stead was allowed to take away his convict outfit and he wore it every Christmas from 1886 on, or so he claimed. However, the aftermath of the Maiden Tribute scandal was not so kind to others who became unwittingly involved in it.

The first casualty was the French midwife Madame Mourez who examined Eliza in Milton Street. For her part in Stead's enactment of a virgin sacrifice she was given six months with hard labour and committed to Millbank Penitentiary. She died a few weeks later sick with bronchitis and pneumonia. At the inquest it was said that she could not cope with her first task of "picking a pound and a half of coir (a fibre derived from coconuts)a day" and she was allowed to knit instead. Her friends who visited her believed her to be 74 years old. After a few days in the Millbank infirmary she expired, the coroner recording a verdict of "natural death".

Though Dr Heywood Smith did not face any criminal charges for carrying out what was essentially the same procedure which sent Madame Mourez to jail, he was severely reprimanded by Judge Lopes. The judge reminded the jury of what he called "the ghastly spectacle" of Eliza's examination in the early hours of the morning in Miss Hutchinson's house. It was no excuse that the doctor believed Eliza had been "bought"; there was no good reason for the the examination he carried out and what he did was a great discredit to the medical profession.

After the trial Dr Heywood Smith faced further censure. As a distinguished physician his livelihood was to a large extent dependent on patronage, and his position as a gynaecologist at the British Lying-in Hospital in Endell Street, Bloomsbury gave him great cache. Like other consultants working for voluntary hospitals at the time he was not paid a salary but his position would ensure his reputation with the hospital governors who included many local dignitaries. They would ensure he had a lucrative private practice.

After Dr Heywood Smith's appearance at the Old Bailey, the Governors met on 19th November to consider his position. A motion was put foward which stated:

> "That in consequence of Dr Heywood Smith's conduct in the case of Eliza Armstrong, so strongly animadverted on by the Judge at the trial, this meeting is of the opinion that in the interests of the charity he should be removed from the medical staff of the hospital."

A special meeting of the Governors had been called and they resolved that, unless Dr Heywood Smith was "removed", they would resign. He had his defenders, however, and a decision was delayed until the Governors learned of the judgement of the British Genealogical Society, of which Dr Heywood Smith was the Secretary. After the trial, the doctor had tendered his resignation, and the Society had regretfully accepted it as he had committed a "grave professional error" when he agreed to the examination of Eliza for which there was no medical justification. This was also the judgement of the British Lying-in Hospital which dismissed him, regretting that they felt it necessary to deal with his "indiscretion" so severely.

A month later, Dr Heywood Smith's membership of the Royal College of Physicians was in serious jeopardy as his conduct in the Armstrong case was considered by the Board of Censors. He had apologised unreservedly for his error of judgement and his failure to verify Stead's claim that he was Eliza's guardian. After a heated debate the College resolved to allow him to remain a member, but issued a severe reprimand read out by the President:

141

> "Speaking generally, and without regard to this special case… it is, in the opinion of the College, a grave professional and moral offence for any physician to examine physically a young girl, even at the request of a parent, without first having satisfied himself that some decided medical good is likely to accrue to the patient from the examination, and also without having first explained to the parent or legal guardian of the girl the inadvisability of such examinations in general and the special objections that exist to their being made. Moreover, the College feels that a young girl should on no consideration be examined excepting in the presence of a matron of mature age, and, as far as the physician can know, of good moral character."

Dr Heywood Smith's chaperone on the night he examined Eliza had been the avowed former brothel keep Rebecca Jarrett.

Dr Heywood Smith gradually regained his reputation as a respected gynaecologist, then a relatively new medical specialism, and died at the grand old age of 91 in 1928.

Mr Mussabini (Sampson Jacques), whose nationality, past and subsequent career all remained a mystery, served his sentence and disappeared. Rebecca Jarrett survived her time in jail but struggled to give up her old ways, returning to drink and her former underworld haunts. The Salvation Army coaxed her back, sending her to America for a while, and she settled down to work at an Army hostel in Mare Street, Hackney. She was there when she died in 1928, by which time she was regarded by the Army as a heroine. The *War Cry* gave her a glowing obituary and offered the public another bowdlerised version of events:

> "… to the amazement and horror of thousands of Englishmen, Stead, Bramwell Booth, and Rebecca Jarrett, with others, had to stand their trial for breaking the very law which their effort had brought into being. They had abducted a girl! It was nothing that she was

carefully shielded throughout the whole of the transaction, and that Mr. Stead had openly declared this action was necessary in order to expose the vilest traffic imaginable. These champions of the helpless—Stead and Rebecca Jarrett—were sent to jail, Stead for three months and Rebecca for six. The General and those involved with him in the case were acquitted. All honour to those who shared in this notable victory!"

Of Rebecca the *War Cry* obituary stated:

"Again and again she almost yielded to despair. Mrs. Bramwell Booth, Mrs. Josephine Butler, and others, spent hours with her in her terrible battles with discouragement and other evils. Their prayers, their love, and faith prevailed, and by the blessing of God she conquered. For a time this redeemed soul assisted in the rescue of girls and women and helped generally in Mrs. Butler's home. Long ago, however, she returned to Mrs. Booth's care and was comfortably accommodated at 259 Mare Street, Hackney, and was thoroughly at home there until the day of her death...

Her last message was: 'Give Mrs. Booth all my love: tell her I'm ready and I'm going Home.' Her General had already written of her, 'She has done well.' Now she has entered into the joy of her Lord and heard His. 'Well, done.' The funeral service in Abney Park Cemetery, on Thursday afternoon, was conducted by Commissioner Lamb...

The newspapers of the Metropolis, where these epic scenes had been enacted, told of her promotion to Glory, described the joyful scenes at the graveside, and, in retelling the stories of the days of the Maiden Tribute, showed how God is using our Army to effect His glorious purposes in the world."

In the immediate aftermath of the trial and the jailing of the conspirators, it looked as if Eliza and her family might fare well. A few days after the end of the Old Bailey trial, the following letter was printed in the *Times* under the heading THE ARMSTRONG CASE:

"Sir—Since the conclusion of this case several persons have said to me 'Are you not now going to do something for the Armstrongs after all the trouble and anxiety they have had in this matter?' I need scarcely say that no public money can be applied for their benefit; but as I know there are many persons who would be glad to give small sums if they were satisfied that the money would be prudently applied, will you kindly allow me, through the medium of The Times, to state that I shall be willing to receive any money sent to me on their behalf?

Charles Armstrong and his wife are both hard-working people, and I will use the money so as to enable them to get a better home, and also to assist them in bringing up their family as they have hitherto done, respectably and in habits of industry. Charles Armstrong was for nearly 21 years in the Militia, and was discharged in consequence of weak eyes in August, 1884, with a certificate of character 'very good'. I will personally acknowledge the receipt of any money that may be sent to me, and I shall consider that I have absolute discretion to deal with the fund as I may think best.

I do not propose to publish a list of subscribers, as my object is simply to give a helping hand to the Armstrong family, and not to encourage any expression of opinion on a case which has been finally dealt with in the due course of the law. Your obedient servant, Harry Bodkin Poland, 5 Paper-buildings, Temple EC."

This appeal bore fruit, for Mr Poland Q.C., was able to report towards the end of December that a "considerable sum" had already been raised. A short report in the *Times* stated:

"Eliza Armstrong was last week placed in the Princess Louise's Home, at Wanstead, for the protection and training of young girls. It is intended to give her two-and-a-half year's good schooling and training, and then to get her into service. The funds will already admit of a fair dowry being presented to her when she comes of age, or of the money being invested at interest for her future support. Her father, on Friday last, was presented, out of the funds, with two new sets of sweeping machines capable of reaching the tops of the highest chimneys built. Mr Poland has further apportioned a part of the funds to furnish the family a new house, and also to insure for them the payment of the extra rent for the first 12 months."

Reporting this a few week's before Christmas 1885 *Lloyd's Weekly Newspaper* said that a number of women had offered to adopt Eliza and she had been made a "very remunerative offer" to appear for a season in Music Hall. However, her parents had visited the Princess Louise Home in Wansted and preferred for her to go there. Over the next two years there are reports of Eliza doing well. The last record that has come to light says that she had taken a job in service. But it does not say where or when. Sadly we do not know what became of Eliza Armstrong. Stead said he had received a letter from her at one time in which she said she was happily married with six children. It was the sort of documentary evidence you would think he would have made public. But if it ever existed it seems to have disappeared from his archives.

There is a little more about Eliza's parents. In January 1886, Charles Armstrong was fined for hitting a woman who had been annoying him. Mrs Armstrong continued to get into drunken brawls and on one occasion in 1888 she was sent to jail for two weeks. She had assaulted a neighbour and kicked a police constable. In her defence her solicitor told the court that since the "unfortunate case" of Eliza Armstrong she had been subjected to "systematic annoyance" with the suggestion that she had sold her daughter for £5. Charles Armstrong, said the solicitor, "had been so worried that he had lost his reason and was now in Marylebone Infirmary." Despite the promise of a new home, it seems Mrs Armstrong still lived in Charles Street.

On 1 August 1886 *Lloyd's Weekly Newspaper* reported that Eliza and her parents were suing Stead, Bramwell Booth and Dr Heywood Smith for damages. There were six claims in all amounting to £7,200. The largest of these was for £1000 made by Eliza against Stead for libel, assault and false imprisonment and against the owners of the *Pall Mall Gazette* for a further £1000. Mr Armstrong was claiming £500 from Stead for libel and a further £500 for the loss of his daughter's services. Mrs Armstrong was claiming £700 from Stead for libel. Both made similar claims against Bramwell Booth and Eliza sought damages from him for assault and wrongful imprisonment. Eliza was also claiming £100 from Dr Heywood Smith for assault. The Armstrongs were encouraged in their pursuit of Stead, Booth, Heywood Smith and the *Pall Mall Gazette* by the success of Nancy Broughton who had sued for libel as she had been described as procuress. According to *Lloyd's Weekly* Mrs Broughton had been paid £200 but she had fallen ill and died in June 1886. Her husband, 'Bash', was continuing with the action.

The newspaper reports on these actions peter out and it is not certain what money was paid out. But it seems very likely that the *Gazette*, Stead and the others settled out of court. Mr Poland was approached for his opinion on the actions and said he would not interfere but he thought it would be wrong to offer money from his appeal fund for legal expenses. Whatever the outcome of these actions, they give a lie to Stead's persistent claim that he would have got off the hook if it had been shown that

Charles Armstrong was not Eliza's legal child. He makes absolutely no mention of being sued by the family or by the Broughton's in his later accounts of the Maiden Tribute affair.

In a brilliant portrait of Stead in his book *After Puritanism* published in 1929, Hugh Kingsmill, the novelist, essayist and biographer wrote:

"The distaste inspired in the ordinary man by crusaders against self-indulgence, and especially by crusaders against sexual self-indulgence, derives from the feeling that this crusading is itself a form of self-indulgence, entered into primarily to satisfy instincts which the mass of men satisfy by less disingenuous methods. To the average sensual man, lacking both in enterprise and imagination, it seemed unfair that Stead should have been rewarded for his varied and curious experiences in houses of ill-fame by the benediction of venerable prelates and the passionate applause of countless refined women.

Opinions may differ about this aspect of Stead's campaign, but it is difficult to find any excuse for the part in the drama thrust upon Mrs Armstrong by Stead and the Salvation Army. If we accept Stead's version, the poverty of Mrs Armstrong was used to force her to sell her daughter for immoral purposes. A campaign on behalf of morality opened with, in the kind of phraseology used by Stead, the ruin of a woman's soul. If we accept Mrs Armstrong's version, she was tricked into appearing before the world, and among her neighbours, as a mother who had sold her daughter into a brothel. Nor can we set much value on Stead's feeling for the self-respect or even ordinary human instincts of the poor, when we find him referring in the following terms to Mrs Armstrong's attempt to recover the daughter transported to Paris by the Salvation Army:

'The mother of Eliza Armstrong, although she might have been willing to sell her daughter into shame, had not bargained for losing her daughter altogether.' "

Chapter Eighteen
The white slave trade

Stead's Maiden Tribute investigation was one of many exposés of prostitution in London in the nineteenth century. However, it was unique in a number of respects. The most significant difference between his journalistic exploration of the underworld and the more sober inquiries conducted by committees in Parliament was his belief that working class mothers routinely sold their daughters to brothels. He had only hearsay evidence for this and one of his chief informants had proved himself to be a very unreliable witness.

Following an investigation into the entrapment of English girls in Belgian brothels, a House of Lords select committee was formed in 1881 to examine the "law relating to the protection of young girls." One of the witnesses was Mr C. E. Howard Vincent who had the grand title of Director of Criminal Investigations at Scotland Yard. Lord Salisbury, who was in the chair, asked Vincent if his attention had been called to the subject of juvenile prostitution in London, to which he replied: "Very much so indeed." Salisbury asked if "juvenile" meant prostitution of girls under 21, and whether it prevailed largely in London. Vincent replied confidently: "In no city in Europe to so large an extent, in my opinion". Down to what age? "Down to the statutory limit of 13", said Vincent, pointing out that there was no protection for girls at that age or older.

Though he appeared to be speaking with the authority of a man who had spent his working life on the streets of London, Vincent was not, properly speaking, a policeman at all and he was forced to admit that he had no first hand experience of the work of prostitutes in the capital. Born into an aristocratic family in 1849, he travelled widely in Europe as a young man and spoke French, German and

Russian. One of his godfathers was Cardinal Manning. After studying at the military college of Sandhurst he took a Commission in the Royal Welch Fusiliers and worked as a war correspondent for the *Daily Telegraph*. Vincent was engaged intermittently as a reporter.

In 1876 he became a barrister, joining the south-eastern circuit of the Probate, Divorce and Admiralty Division of the High Court. At each stage in his career he published books on his latest interest and he continued to work as a journalist for the *Daily Telegraph*. In 1877 he went to Paris where he studied the workings of the police, writing a report on the work of the French detectives. It was this that got him the post of Director of Criminal Investigation at Scotland Yard. He set out to reform the Metropolitan Police, and, in 1882, wrote 'A Police Code and Manual of Criminal Law'. To encourage a higher quality of detective work he introduced the Howard Vincent Cup, an annual prize of 100 guineas for the best piece of detective work. But whatever his other qualities, Vincent was an odd choice as a witness for an inquiry into child prostitution.

Though he had no personal knowledge of the vice trade, Vincent told the House of Lords Select Committee he had consulted two of his officers who patrolled the St James's area and Pimlico.

> "There are houses in London, in many parts of London, where there are people who will procure children for the purposes of immorality and prostitution, without any difficulty whatsoever above the age of 13, children without number at 14, 15 and 16 years of age. Superintendent Dunlap will tell you that juvenile prostitution is rampant at this moment, and that in the streets about the Haymarket, Waterloo Place and Piccadilly, from nightfall these are children of 14, 15 and 16 years of age going about openly soliciting prostitution."

If that was not shocking enough, Vincent continued:

> "Now it constantly happens, and I believe in the generality of cases it is so, that these children live at home; this prostitution actually takes place with the knowledge and connivance of the mother and to the profit of the household. I am speaking of some facts within my knowledge, from hearsay, of course, but I have no reason to doubt them. These procuresses, or whatever you may call them, have an understanding with the mother of the girl that she shall come to that house at a certain hour, and the mother perfectly well knows for what purpose she goes there, and it is with her knowledge and connivance, and with her consent, that the girl goes."

When he was asked by Salisbury whether the children went out to walk the streets from their own homes, Vincent said he did not know. It became evident, in fact, that Vincent had very little hard information for the committee. Asked if these children could get lodgings he said he thought not. So how did they ply their trade? They would go to coffee houses with men and obtain a bed. Vincent insisted that most child prostitutes had mothers who not only knew what they were doing but took money from them. In the first instance they might be given work in public house or a "brothel" (ie lodging house) and would be introduced to a life of vice in that way.

Such was the scale of prostitution in London, said Vincent, that it was "impossible for any respectable woman to walk from the top of the Haymarket to Wellington Street, Strand after three o'clock in the afternoon." The Strand was "crowded" with prostitutes and after midnight there might be 500 soliciting on the streets between Piccadilly Circus and the bottom of Waterloo-place.

The police, however, were powerless to stop it. Soliciting was only an offence, said Vincent, if it was: "to the annoyance and obstruction of passengers and no respectable person is willing to go into a police court and say they were solicited by prostitutes."

It is clear from the transcript of the committee's questioning of Vincent that the members were not convinced he knew what he was talking about. At one point he said: "... the police have so little power of dealing with prostitutes or brothels, that they know very little about them."

He was quite sure most young girls were put on the street with the knowledge of their mothers though he was not able to tell the committee how he knew that. In fact when he was reminded that he had said that it was very common for mothers to facilitate the debauchery of their children he replied: "I do not state it as a fact, but as my strong belief."

It was this view of the nature of prostitution in London that was to greatly influence Stead when he was conducting his Maiden Tribute investigation four years later, in 1885. Stead consulted Vincent who told him that he could not add anything to what he had told the House of Lords in 1881. What he did not mention was the fact that a second sitting of the House of Lords Select Committee had heard evidence from witnesses much more knowledgeable than Vincent who flatly contradicted his opinions.

There was a difficulty finding reliable information about the scale and nature of prostitution but the Select Committee had done their best to weigh up the evidence. There was, for example, a set of statistics compiled by "the Chaplain of one of Her Majesty's prisons" giving the social background of more than 3,000 convicted prostitutes from both London and the Country. They were not, evidently, a very devout sample: only 68 still attended church while 588 had never been to church or Sunday School and were described as "quite ignorant and heathen". Of 3,064 prostitutes only 371 could "read and write fairly", 1,016 could "read and write imperfectly", 464 could read only and 1,213 were illiterate.

Half the prostitutes were orphans while nearly a thousand had only one parent. More than half had been, or still were, domestic servants while more than 800 were described as machinists, boxmakers, tailoresses, laundresses, costers etc. There were 44 "women of a better class" and fewer than a hundred widows, needlewomen, barmaids, and dressmakers. A few were married and supporting their husbands by prostitution, others were married but separated or deserted. Asked to give "the age at which they were seduced" three said 11, five the age of 12, and sixteen said they were 13 years old. The commonest ages given were between seventeen and twenty-two.

Asked about "the immediate cause of their State"—that is to say, what it was led them into prostitution—the largest number replied that it was something they simply chose to do. Only eleven said it was to support their mothers, while thirty five said they were supporting "lazy husbands". More than 800 said they had been "seduced under promise of marriage" and another 360 that they had been living with a man who deserted them. Fewer than 500 said they had been "led away" by companions or decoy girls, and only 164 said they had become prostitutes because of poverty or lack of work.

A very knowledgeable witness, who had had a long and varied career in rescue work, flatly contradicted Vincent on the critical question of whether or not girls were encouraged to become prostitutes by their mothers. Ellice Hopkins, the daughter of a Cambridge mathematics tutor, devoted her life to a variety of "missions" with which she hoped to save the souls of those living a godless existence. In 1860, when she was just twenty-four years old, Hopkins had a hall built near Cambridge where she preached to working men and brought them in in their hundreds. The death of her father, to whom she was devoted, so affected her that she abandoned the work in Cambridge and moved to Brighton in Sussex. Here she became involved in various groups who were working to rescue prostitutes.

Hopkins was involved in many missions and movements before she took a special interest in the plight of girls who were being raised in circumstances which made them especially vulnerable to seduction and a life of prostitution. She managed to get an amendment to the Industrial Schools Act which would enable magistrates to take girls away from bawdy houses or other places where they might be corrupted and place them in reformatory schools.

This Act was of special interest to the House of Lords Select Committee, as was the first hand knowledge Hopkins had acquired of the circumstances of juvenile prostitution.

She was disappointed that the amendment she had fought for had had little effect because magistrates were reluctant to take children away from the mothers even if they were being raised in a brothel. However, Hopkins told the Committee:

> "I wish to state that having personal experience of what leads …young girls to join the outcast class of prostitutes, I must contradict Mr Vincent's opinion, that the large majority of mothers send their children out to prostitution; I can only say, emphatically, it is no such thing; I have known cases of it, we have all known cases, where a mother has sent her own children into the streets to earn money in that nefarious manner; they are only exceptional cases."

Quite a number of girls who turned to prostitution, said Hopkins, had been seduced by a man who said he would marry them and had been left to care for a baby that they could not afford to feed and clothe on a typical wage of £16 a year. "But the most extensive cause of all which led to the greatest number of girls going astray," she told the Committee, "is that they get entangled with girls who are already lost; those girls have a strong tendency to try and pull others down to their own miserable level... they have on the one hand a life of drudgery... they have on the other hand, the sight of finery and luxury, everything that can act as an inducement to lead them to follow these girls into a life of vice."

Men who seduced girls with offers of money were also to blame: "Stop the money of men" said Hopkins "and in six week's time the whole thing would be starved out."

Once again contradicting the claims of police witnesses that mothers were often responsible for the corruption of girls, Hopkins said curtly: "A large proportion of these girls we find are motherless, and therefore no mothers to be implicated in it."

As to the age of young prostitutes she confirmed the impression of others that it was falling, and she could cite several cases of girls as young as nine who had come to the notice of rescue workers. Stead's belief that working class mothers routinely sold their children to brothels had no foundation. It was Howard Vincent who had persuaded him it was true. And it was the reformer Josephine Butler who gave him the idea that the sale of children was analogous to that of the sale of slaves in the Southern States of America. The possibility that there might not be a market in virgins never seems to have crossed Stead's mind.

Rebecca Jarrett had never claimed that she procured girls by buying them from their mothers. When Stead asked her to do this for his Secret Commission he had set her an impossible task. The only way Jarrett could fulfil her commission was by pretending she had bought a girl. About the only doubt Stead ever had was whether or not Jarrett had lied to him about how she came to spirit Eliza away from her mother.

The jury at the Old Bailey had said that they felt Stead had been misled by his "agent". They did not believe Jarrett had bought Eliza.

So what did happen in Charles Street on the day after Derby Day in 1885?

Chapter Nineteen
The deal

Rebecca Jarrett had made several attempts to find Stead a girl, or girls, before she visited her friend Nancy Broughton. For one reason or another she had failed to deliver. But Stead would not let her off the hook and bullied her. It is likely that she decided the only way she could get a girl would be to visit her friend Nancy and to explain to her what her mission was. If she could help find a girl of the right age there would be a bit of money for her, and for the girl's family. Nancy need not worry about the girl's well being because the person who had commissioned her was only going to pretend that she was being sold on to a brothel. The girl would only be away for a few days and then she could go back to her mother. Jarrett herself would care for her until she was home.

When Eliza heard about the possibility of getting a post as a maid she was very excited. It seems it was she who persuaded her mother to let her go. It is probable Mrs Armstrong did not know about Jarrett's proposal to Nancy, but Nancy could reassure her that Eliza would be well looked after and would write to her. In that sense, it would be true to say that it was Nancy Broughton who 'sold' Eliza to Jarrett. The evidence is that she got more of the money Stead had given Jarrett than Mrs Armstrong.

It is unlikely Jarrett knew that Stead planned to have Eliza examined by the French mid-wife. However, it would have been difficult for her not to go along with it as she would have to admit that the girl was not really sold by her mother. When, in the brothel in Poland Street, Jarrett was unable to get Eliza to give the chloroform a "good sniff up", she must have been terrified about what she had got herself in to.

As Eliza became more and more disorientated and alarmed she clung to Jarrett. After the night in

Nottingham Place, where Dr Heywood Smith examined her, Eliza would not leave Jarrett's side. It is quite clear Jarrett had no idea that Stead planned to send the girl to France. In fact Stead almost certainly decided on this course of action when he realised that there was a possibility that Eliza might get free and give an account of what she had been subjected to. Eliza's fearful and tearful refusal to let Mrs Combe take her away meant that Jarrett had to go to Paris to make sure Eliza did not run away.

At the Old Bailey Jarrett accused Stead of breaking his promise to her that she could have any girls after he had done with them. This was important to Jarrett because it was almost certainly her plan to return Eliza to Charles Street once she had served Stead's purpose. Josephine Butler also accused Stead of breaking a promise to her when he sent Eliza abroad. So Jarrett could not stick to the agreement she had reached with Nancy Broughton, who understandably became very anxious when she realised Eliza had not been returned home as planned. That is why she was so agitated when she was first contacted by the reporter from *Lloyd's Weekly*.

At one point in the trial at the Old Bailey Stead was asked why Eliza was moved from Paris to Loriol-sur-Drome. Bramwell Booth appears to have taken responsibility for that. Questioned about this at the Old Bailey the reason for this sudden decision was that there might be an attempt by Rebecca Jarrett and her "friends" to take Eliza back to England. Booth had heard from Josephine Butler that Hope Cottage had been attacked and that she feared for Rebecca's safety.

> "I sent instructions by telegram to take the child away to Loriol, because that morning I had seen Mrs Josephine Butler who told me that the Sullivans, and so on, were down at Winchester harassing Rebecca—I was under the impression that the Broughtons, whom I knew then or by that time, had learnt, had sold the

child, were friends of Rebecca before, and I thought that if Rebecca yielded to temptation to go back to her old life, one of the first things would be that they would try to get this poor child back, consequently I was very anxious to get the child to an address that she did not know, because I knew she knew where she was in Paris."

Booth said he was not influenced by the fact that the day he decided Eliza would have to be moved was the very same day Mrs Armstrong had applied to the police-court to look for her daughter, the 11th July. He knew nothing about that. If he had known, he said:

"I do not think it would have influenced me in sending the child away, because I knew that if the mother made a formal demand upon me for the child I had no claim to it, and it would have been perfectly childish for me to send it away from Paris merely for the sake of hiding it from its mother, because I knew its mother would come to me."

Booth seems to have forgotten that, while giving evidence at Bow Street, he admitted he had threatened to make Eliza a "ward of chancery" if the mother insisted on her return. He had done so in the presence of Inspector Borner.

When Eliza wrote to her mother from Paris, Stead decided not to forward the letter. The reason he gave was that he thought Eliza would be in danger of being "sold again" if she was in touch with her mother. It is much more likely that he was fearful that Eliza would tell her mother what had happened to her and he would be in trouble. The next letter Eliza wrote was sent from the family she had been placed with in the South of France and was duly delivered. Had Booth and the Army erred by sending Eliza to a household that was not in their sway? Mrs Combe was in the Salvation Army, but her brother in Loriol-sur-Drome was not. Or did they allow Eliza's second letter to be delivered to her mother because by then they knew the game was up? The police were by then demanding that they be given the address to which Eliza had been sent.

Though much of Stead's account of the sale of Lily was fiction the little bit of reality he allowed in to the story was, as it happened, his undoing. His brief interview with Eliza in which she told him about her trips to Richmond and Epping, the oblique reference to the names of streets, and the mention of Derby Day, were enough to suggest that Lily was the same girl as Eliza Armstrong. Had he not offered those clues Eliza might have spent the rest of her life in France and never seen her parents and brothers and sisters again. Which is what Stead wanted. Happily Eliza not only escaped that fate but, through her extraordinary adventure, became unwittingly the inspiration for the creation of one of the most endearing characters in twentieth century theatre: George Bernard Shaw's Eliza Doolittle.

Chapter Twenty
Eliza immortalised

At the time of the Maiden Tribute furore in July 1885, George Bernard Shaw had just begun to write unsigned book reviews for the *Pall Mall Gazette*. He was, at first, a keen supporter of Stead's campaign and when he learned that the newsagent W. H. Smith had banned the *Gazette* because of the Maiden Tribute stories he wrote to Stead offering to help sell copies on the street. His letter to Stead was ignored but he was very familiar with the story and the furore it created. However, the revelations at Bow Street and the Old Bailey which exposed the 'Lily' story as a fake, or "put up job", as Shaw himself described it, he lost respect for Stead.

'We all felt that if ever a man deserved six months' imprisonment Stead deserved it for such a betrayal of our confidence in him.'

In the years after the Maiden Tribute scandal Shaw became a well-established playwright. He regarded the theatre as a vehicle for social reform as well as satire and this frequently got him in to trouble with the official government censor, the Lord Chamberlain's Office, which licensed all plays. Stead had been brought up in a north country manse where he was taught that the theatre was the "Devil's Chapel" and he espoused the cause of the National Vigilance Association which campaigned for stricter censorship on the stage. This must have been a huge annoyance for Shaw as it has been calculated that one tenth of all the plays banned between 1895 and 1909 were written by him. This included his *Mrs Warren's Profession* and *Press Cuttings*.

When Shaw read the reports of Stead's death on the *Titanic*, and the obituaries which followed, he would have been reminded of the story of 'Lily' in the Maiden

Tribute investigation of 1885 and his disgust when he realised it was largely fictional.

There are no reliable reports of Stead's last hours on the stricken liner. Some had him clinging to a raft with John Jacob Astor before slipping in to the icy water. Others that he refused to get into a lifeboat. One that he was seen praying serenely. There appeared to be a will to have Stead die the death of a martyr. Perhaps this rankled with Shaw for he began to weave many elements of the Maiden Tribute into the play he was finishing in April 1912—*Pygmalion*.

It is quite surprising that the degree to which this most popular of Shaw's plays draws on and satirises Stead's story of the sale of the cockney girl to a brothel has only recently been studied in any depth. However, a brilliant analysis entitled 'Parodying the £5 Virgin: Bernard Shaw and the Playing of *Pygmalion*', published in the *Yale Journal of Criticism* in 2000 reveals not only some very obvious digs at the Maiden Tribute but some more subtle references as well. The author, Celia Marshik, makes the point that Shaw could not really attack Stead outright so soon after the Titanic disaster but "as the playright finished *Pygmalion* in May and June of that year, a gentle parody was the most he might tactfully direct at the sainted Stead."

In the first instance, there are the blatant references to the £5 virgin. The play's heroine is Eliza and she comes from Lisson Grove. So Eliza Armstrong is a model for the flower girl Eliza Doolittle. Whereas the real Eliza's father was a chimney sweep, Shaw has Mr Doolittle as a dustman and one of the "undeserving poor". Not a bad description of Stead's judgement on the people of Charles Street, Lisson Grove. When Mr Doolittle tracks his daughter down to the home of Professor Higgins who is trying to get her to speak like a Duchess he asks for £5 for his daughter. She is not much use to him so he might as well sell her off.

Although *Pygmalion*, and the stage and film versions titled *My Fair Lady*, is very light-hearted, Marshik finds many sinister references to the original £5 virgin story told by Stead. From the outset, Eliza Doolittle is anxious that she should be considered virtuous and she is wary of the intentions of "gentlemen". The play opens with a group of people sheltering from the rain in the wide portico of the Inigo Jones church in Covent Garden. Eliza tries to get one of them, a Colonel Pickering, to buy her flowers. She and the others notice that there is a man who appears to be making notes about everything she says. Fearing that he is a "copper's nark" (a police informer) she asks to see what he has written. He has to read it out for her.

"Cheer ap, Keptin; n' baw ya flahr orf a pore gel." Eliza is distraught: "It's because I called him Captain. I meant no harm. [To the gentleman] Oh, sir, don't let him lay a charge agen me for a word like that. You—"

The gentleman she has called "Captain" says she meant no harm, and the various by-standers begin to close in on the man.

It is then revealed that he is a phoneticist, Professor Higgins, who has astonishing knowledge of local accents. That person is clearly from Selsey, that one from Hoxton. Of Eliza Doolittle Professor Higgins asked: "How do you come to be up so far east? You were born in Lisson Grove." Startled, she retorts: "Oh, what harm is there in my leaving Lisson Grove? It wasn't fit for a pig to live in; and I had to pay four-and-six a week." She then begins to cry.

When Eliza Doolittle, intrigued by Higgins and with money from "the gentleman" pursues them in a cab, and asks to be taught to speak properly, she remains defensive and suspicious. Higgins at first says: "Why, this is the girl I jotted down last night. She's no use: I've got all the records I want of the Lisson Grove lingo; and I'm not going to waste another cylinder on it."

When he relents and agrees to take on the challenge of turning her into a lady, he tells his housekeeper to take the clothes she is in and to burn them. Eliza is shocked: "You're no gentleman, you're not, to talk of such things. I'm a good girl, I am; and I know what the like of you are, I do." To which Higgins responds: "We want none of your Lisson Grove prudery here, young woman. You've got to learn to behave like a duchess. Take her away, Mrs. Pearce. If she gives you any trouble wallop her."

It is possible to imagine Shaw chuckling to himself as he penned these lines, the working class Eliza Doolittle offended by the forwardness of Higgins, who treats her with disdain and who might just have sexual designs on her. Mrs Pearce, the housekeeper, is not too sure about what these gentleman want with a rough flower girl. When Higgins offers Eliza a chocolate she is hesitant: "How do I know what might be in them? I've heard of girls being drugged by the like of you." To reassure her, Higgins cuts the chocolate in two, and pops one half into his own mouth.

So here is Eliza from Lisson Grove, more or less at the mercy of the highbrow Professor Higgins, worried about being drugged. A highlight of the play is the confrontation between Eliza's father, Mr Doolittle and Professor Higgins. At first Higgins first tells Mr Doolittle to take his daughter away, fearing that her coming to his house is a set-up so the father can blackmail him. But he becomes fascinated by Doolittle's gift of the gab, and then understands that all the father wants is a small payment.

Mr Doolittle puts it like this: "Well, the truth is, I've taken a sort of fancy to you, Governor; and if you want the girl, I'm not so set on having her back home again but what I might be open to an arrangement. Regarded in the light of a young woman, she's a fine handsome girl. As a daughter she's not worth her keep; and so I tell you straight. All I ask is my rights as a father; and you're the last man alive to expect me to let her go for nothing; for I can see you're one of the straight sort, Governor. Well, what's a five pound note to you? And what's Eliza to me?"

When Higgins appears outraged that Doolittle is prepared to sell his daughter, apparently for immoral purposes, Doolittle says that the price for that would be nearer £50. Higgins offers £10, but Doolittle will have no more than the £5 he initially asked for. Happy with the deal, and announcing with cheerful confidence that the whole of the fee will be spent "by Monday", the dustman Doolittle exits this early scene without ever asking what Higgins wants with Eliza.

These farcical circumstances echo some of the absurdities of Eliza Armstrong's real-life drama and are not much more far-fetched than Stead's imaginary recreation of what happened in Lisson Grove in June 1885. In a note attached to *Pygmalion*, Shaw refuses to speculate on what happens to Eliza Doolittle after she has been successfully turned into a well-spoken lady. Similarly we have no account of what became of Eliza Armstrong after her brief initiation into respectable life. No doubt her spelling improved, and some of the rough edges were knocked off her speech. She was at least re-incarnated as *My Fair Lady*.

Chapter Twenty-one
Stead: in memoriam

Born in 1849 in Northumberland, the son of a devout Congregationalist minister, Stead had very little formal education and began work as a clerk filling in order books for a Russian merchant in Newcastle-upon-Tyne. To amuse himself he wrote letters to the editor of the leading newspaper of the region *The Northern Echo* published in Darlington.

Stead's steady correspondence with the indulgent editor of the *Echo* concerned such issues as the need to create a Charity Organisation Society to prevent "indiscriminate almsgiving". Encouraged to write more and hone his journalistic skills, Stead became a regular contributor to the newspaper. Then, out of the blue, the editor resigned and the owners offered Stead the job. He had never been in a newspaper office and went off to study journalism with an editor in Leeds. After this crash course he took up his post in Darlington in 1871 at the age of twenty-two. From the outset he regarded newspapers as propaganda sheets and thought his own tenure would be a "wonderful way of attacking the devil".

Rather than concentrating on local news, Stead began a series of campaigns to influence government policy on everything from "Bulgarian atrocities" to the cause of Russian Tsars. He sent copies of the *Echo* to the leading politicians of the day and became an acquaintance of Gladstone. By sheer effort and effrontery he became a familiar figure, a man anyone with a just cause could turn to for publicity. Two years after taking over at the *Echo* he married Emma Lucy Wilson and they soon had children which arrived at regular intervals. He was, in short, a man of some substance by the time he was in his late twenties.

Stead always expressed great respect and affection for his parents and to have thrived on a Puritan upbringing that would have driven most children to despair. In his father's north country manse, he wrote,

> "a severe interdict was laid upon all time-wasting amusements... Among them in my youth three stood conspicuous from the subtlety of their allurement, and the deadly results which followed yielding to their seductions. The first was the Theatre, which was the Devil's Chapel; the second was Cards, which were the Devil's Prayer Book; and the third was the Novel, which was regarded as a kind of Devil's Bible, whose meretricious attractions waged an unholy competition against the reading of God's Word."

Stead did not smoke and he was a teetotaller. His only vice was an intense interest in sex. He befriended Josephine Butler the campaigner for women's rights who opposed the Contagious Diseases Acts on the grounds that they discriminated against women. These laws were passed to control venereal disease in garrison towns and subjected prostitutes to rude examination and persecution while leaving their male clients alone. Stead always expressed a horror at the scale of prostitution in Victorian society, yet privately he was not immune to infidelity. His personal, self-flagellating letters to himself reveal that he almost certainly had an affair with a Russian woman, Madame Novicoff only four years into his marriage. He certainly upset his wife a good deal, though she remained for ever silent on the subject.

This was the man who, having made his mark in Darlington, was ushered into the evil world of London at the invitation of John Morely editor of the distinguished and sober *Pall Mall Gazette*. He became Morley's assistant and languished a while, biding his time. When Morely was elected to Parliament, Stead took over editorial control of the *Gazette* and began his campaigning once again. That was in 1883. He was now in a tremendously powerful position and was happy to turn the newspaper into a campaigning journal. It was he who pressured the government into sending General Gordon to his death in the Sudan in the belief that he could save this outpost of Empire for Britain. He was involved in a campaign to improve the housing of the poor, though he rejected the idea that the working classes should have the vote.

Stead returned to the *Pall Mall Gazette* when he left prison. After a few years he set up his own daily paper, which was not a success, and continued to get involved in national and international campaigns. In the years just before the First World War he became a leading light in an international peace movement. Invited to speak in the United States, where he was a well-known figure, he took the train to Southampton in April 1912 to board the most luxurious liner the world had yet seen.

He had become interested in spiritualism and had, a few years earlier, written a story in which a liner with too few lifeboats is hit by an iceberg. Passengers are saved from the sinking ship by a telepathic message. A few years after his death, his daughter, Estelle published his reports sent from beyond the grave, with one startling revelation: he was wearing the same clothing on the other side as he had been when he went down on the Titanic.

Timeline

The year: 1885

3 June Derby Day: Eliza Armstrong is taken from her home in Lisson Grove by a woman calling herself Mrs Sullivan. She is a friend of the Armstrong's neighbour, Nancy Broughton. It is agreed Eliza will write home every week.

10 June: Nancy receives a letter from her friend Mrs Sullivan (known as Becky) to say Eliza is well and they are in Winchester. There is no letter from Eliza to her mother.

6 July: The *Pall Mall Gazette* publishers a story about a girl of thirteen bought for £5. The girl allegedly sold to a brothel is called Lily.

11 July: Eliza's mother tells the local magistrate that her daughter is missing and she thinks it might be the same girl as in the *Gazette* story. She bursts into tears in the court.

12 July: *Lloyd's Weekly Illustrated* newspaper publishes Mrs Armstrong's story about her lost daughter Eliza. Reporter visits Mrs Armstrong at her home in Charles Street, Lisson Grove and interviews her neighbours Nancy and Jack Broughton.

13 July: *Pall Mall Gazette* prints short version of *Lloyd's Weekly Illustrated* story without comment though Stead knows that the Lily of his story is Eliza Armstrong.

14 July: Inspector Edward Borner, on instructions of the Magistrate, visits Nancy Broughton to begin his search for Eliza. Nancy shows him the letter she received from her friend Becky, alias Mrs Sullivan. It has the address of Hope Cottage, High Cliff, Winchester.

15 July: First of four private meetings of the Mansion House Committee called by Stead to vouch for the accuracy of his reports. Mrs Armstrong attends one of these with Mr Thomas to appeal for the return of her daughter. She weeps. Stead sees her but says nothing.

Meanwhile, Inspector Borner goes to the address given in Mrs Sullivan's letter. There is nobody there but he finds Mrs

Josephine Butler, wife of the Canon of Winchester Cathedral, who is a campaigner for womens' rights and had who set up Hope Cottage as a home for " fallen" women. She tells Borner the Salvation Army is involved in the disappearance of Eliza.

16 July: Inspector Borner calls on Bramwell Booth, Chief of Staff, of the Salvation Army at their headquarters in Queen Victoria Street. Booth says he knows something of the case of Eliza but is not sure where she is. He will forward the address to Scotland Yard when he has it. Inspecter Borner goes on holiday.

1 August: Borner goes back to see Booth as he still has no address for Eliza. Mrs Armstrong goes with him. Booth hands over an address in the South of France.

14 August: Mrs Armstrong receives a letter from Eliza sent from Loriol-sur Drome.

19 August: Eliza's father, Charles, accompanies Inspector Von Turnow to France in the hope of finding the girl and bringing her home.

21 August: Mr Armstrong and Von Turnow discover Eliza is no longer in Loriol-sur-Drome but has been sent back to Paris. While they are in Loriol, Stead is heckled at a meeting in London about the disappearance of Eliza. For the first time he admits he is responsible for taking her from her family and a street he claimed was "steeped in vice".

22 August: Stead writes a letter to Mrs Armstrong to say that he had "been informed for the first time" that she wanted her daughter back. He holds on to it until Eliza's return from France. Eliza spends this Saturday night at Stead's home in Wimbledon.

24 August: Eliza and her mother have a tearful and emotional reunion at Stead's home in Wimbledon. His wife gives them lunch. Stead goes to his office and then on holiday to Switzerland. He is not there for the reunion.

26 August: A warrant is issued for the arrest of Rebecca Jarrett (alias Mrs Sullivan) for the abduction of Eliza and indecent assault. Inspector Borner cannot find her and asks Bramwell Booth to tell him where she is.

30 August: Jarrett gives herself up at Scotland Yard. Warrants are issued for the arrest of W. T. Stead, Sampson Jacques, Bramwell

Booth, Madame Mourez and Madame Combe on various charges relating to the abduction of Eliza and her treatment during Stead's mock sale to a brothel and rape.

2 September: Rebecca Jarrett appears at Bow Street Magistrates Court. Stead hears of this and the warrant for his arrest, and sends a telegram from the Swiss Alps to say he is on his way back to answer all charges.

7 September: The committal proceedings begin at Bow Street with all the accused before the Magistrate Mr. Vaughan.

3 October: All the defendants are committed for trial at the Old Bailey.

7 November: Stead and Jarrett found guilty of the charge of abduction. Charges against Mdme Combe dropped, Booth and Jacques found not guilty.

10 November: A newly sworn jury finds Madame Mourez guilty of indecent assault on Eliza, and Stead, Jacques and Jarrett guilty of aiding and abetting her. Sentences passed on all four.

1886

18 January: W. T. Stead released from Holloway Prison and greeted by a mass meeting of supporters at Exeter Hall in London.

25 December: W. T. Stead celebrates Christmas—the first of many— wearing his old prison uniform.

1912

15 April: W. T. Stead goes down with the Titanic. George Bernard Shaw puts the finishing touches to his play *Pygmalion*.

Stead claimed he regularly wore his old prison uniform at Christmas

A note on sources

By far the most comprehensive account of the abduction of Eliza Armstrong can be found in the cryptic notes recording the proceedings at the Old Bailey where Stead, Jacques, Booth, Jarrett, Mdme Mourez and Mdme Combe were tried. I printed these out at the British Library several years ago. Today I can read them in the comfort of my own home at www.oldbaileyonline.org. A few key words will take you to the relevant sessions.

It was at the Old Bailey that Stead's attempt to justify what he did with and to Eliza Amstrong collapsed under cross examination. Anyone who doubts my interpretation of events can now very easily make their own judgement.

In contrast to the totally unsubstantiated claims made by Stead in his Maiden Tribute of Modern Babylon articles, the Select Committee of the House of Lords Report on the Law Relating to the Protection of Young Girls (1881-1882) collected reliable evidence on the nature and scale of juvenile prostitution in London and elsewhere. One witness rejected outright the notion that mothers commonly sold their daughters to brothels, as Stead believed.

I am indebted to Celia Marshik, Associate Professor of English and Gender Studies at Stony Brook University, New York for revealing the extent to which George Bernard Shaw used to the Maiden Tribute case when putting the finishing touches to *Pygmalion*. We met when she was in London a while back to discuss her paper Parodying the £5 Virgin: Bernard Shaw and the Playing of *Pygmalion* (*The Yale Journal of Criticism* 13, 2000: 321-341.)

A great deal was gleaned from newspapers which covered what was generally known as the "Abduction" story. Among those consulted were *Lloyd's Weekly Newspaper*, the *Daily News*, the *Telegraph*, the *Times*, the *St*

James's Gazette, *Police Weekly Illustrated News*, *Marylebone Mercury*, *War Cry* and, of course, the *Pall Mall Gazette* itself.

Last but not least there is a wealth of information about the Eliza Armstrong case on the Stead Resource Site at www.attackingthedevil.co.uk.

Select bibliography

Bristow, Edward J., *Vice and Vigilance: Purity Movements in Britain since 1700*, Dublin: Gill and Macmillan, 1977

Butler, Josephine, *Personal Reminiscences of a Great Crusade*, London: Horace Marshall & Son, 1896

Jones, Victor Pierce, *Saint or Sensationalist: The Story of W. T. Stead*, Chichester: Gooday, 1988

Jordan, Jane, *Josephine Butler*, London: John Murray, 2001

Kingsmill, Hugh, *After Puritanism* London: Duckworth, 1952

Lloyd, Chris, *Attacking the Devil: 150 Years of the Northern Echo*, Darlington: Northern Echo, 1999

Mearns, Andrew, *The Bitter Cry of Outcast London: an Inquiry into the Condition of the Abject Poor*, London: James Clark & Co, 1883

Plowden, Alison, *The Case of Eliza Armstrong: 'A Child of 13 Bought for £5'*, London: BBC Publications, 1974

Schultz, Raymond L., *Crusader in Babylon: W. T. Stead and the Pall Mall Gazette*, Nebraska: University of Nebraska, 1972

Scott, J. W. Robertson, *The Story of the Pall Mall Gazette*, Oxford: Oxford University Press, 1950

Scott, J. W. Robertson, *The Life and Death of a Newspaper*, London: Methuen, 1952

Simpson, Antony E., ed. *The Maiden Tribute of Modern Babylon*, New Jersey: True Bill Press, 2007

Stead, Estelle W., *My Father: Personal & Spiritual Reminiscences*, London: Thomas Nelson, 1913

Stead, W. T.: *My First Imprisonment*, London: E. Marlborough & Co, 1886

Terrot, Charles, *The Maiden Tribute: A Study of the White Slave Traffic of the Nineteenth Century*, London: Frederick Muller, 1959

Walker, Pamela, *Pulling the Devil's Kingdom Down* University of California Press March 2001

Walkowitz, Judith R., *City of Dreadful Delight: Narratives of Sexual Danger in Late Victorian London*, London: Virago Press, 1994

Weeks, Jeffrey, *Sex, Politics & Society: The Regulation of Sexuality since 1800*, London: Longman, 1981

Weightman, Gavin, *Signor Marconi's Magic Box*, Harper Collins 2003

Whyte, Frederick, *The Life of W.T. Stead*, 2 vols London: Jonathan Cape, 1925

Note: Various spellings of the protagonists can be found in contemporary accounts. Wherever possible the spelling from the Old Bailey court records of the two trials has been used. They can be found at www.oldbaileyonline.org, reference: t18851019-1031, t18851019-1032.

Illustrations

Black and white from *The Illustrated Police News*, 1885

Cover design

Ellie Davies

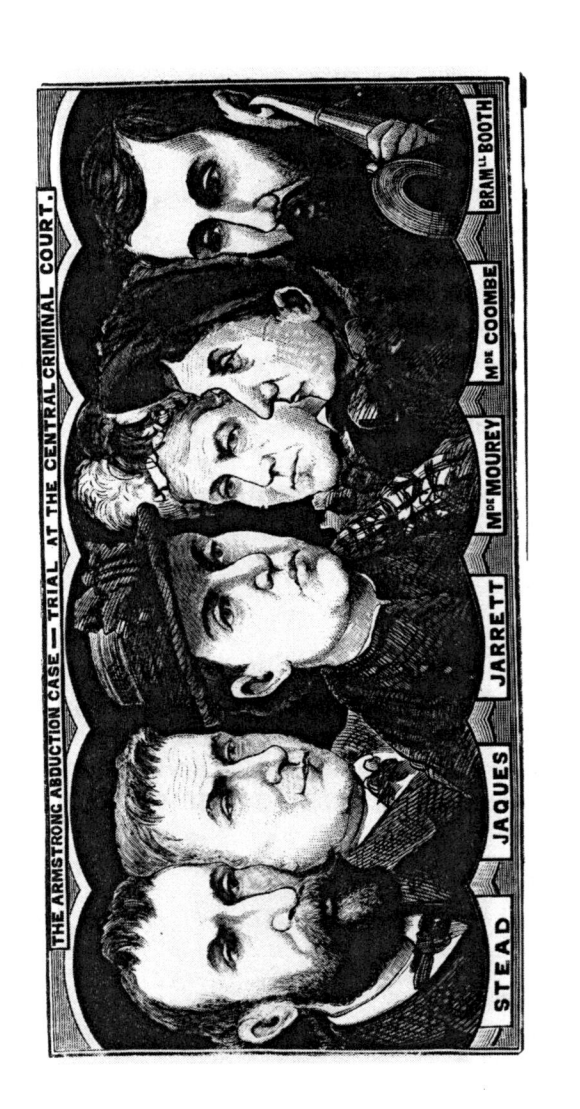

THE ARMSTRONG ABDUCTION CASE — TRIAL AT THE CENTRAL CRIMINAL COURT.

STEAD JAQUES JARRETT M^{de} MOUREY M^{de} COOMBE BRAM^{ll} BOOTH

The Industrial Revolutionaries: the creation of the modern world: 1776-1914

by Gavin Weightman

The big question I set out to answer in this book was: once industrialism began how did this new kind of manufacture and economy spread across the world? Was it inevitable, or did those countries which followed Britain's lead—the United States, Germany, France and Japan—simply import and borrow British technology?

Some key British workers were enticed abroad initially, but by the first half of the nineteenth century British confidence was such that not only was export of expertise allowed, it was encouraged. Towards the end of the nineteenth century the astonishing industrialisation of Japan began. The way in which the Japanese responded to the threat posed by industrial might was one of the most fascinating episodes in the story.

Some young Samurai risked their lives by visiting the West in disguise: Japan forbid any contact with foreigners. The celebrated Choshu Five with their hair cropped and in Western style dress made their way to University College London and eventually back to Japan where they became leaders of the new Meji regime which embraced industrialism with a mad enthusiasm. As early as 1905 Japan was able to defeat Russia in a major war.

The Choshu Five were not themselves inventors: they were promoters of industrialism. And this is a theme that emerges. Those who believed in innovation and drove industry forward were as important as the famous inventors in bringing about industrialisation.

"Weightman expertly marshals his cast of characters across continents and centuries, forging a genuinely global history..."
New York Times

Signor Marconi's Magic Box: The invention that sparked the radio revolution

by Gavin Weightman

When Hertz died tragically in 1894 at the age of just 36 there were many obituaries which described his experimental work. These inspired a number of inventors to see if the laboratory signals could have practical use. One was Marconi, then a 19 year old living on his father's estate near Bologna in Italy.

Though he really had no theory to back his hunch, Marconi believed that he could adapt Herz's apparatus to send Morse Code signals over quite long distances. Using primitive equipment he discovered that his wireless signals could travel at least a mile and appeared to go through or round hills. It was vital that wireless could operate over long distances as one of the great potential markets was ship to shore and Marconi had his eye on the Atlantic liners. He simply ignored the received wisdom that his wireless waves would simply fly off into the atmosphere and would not hug the curved surface of the Earth .

In 1901 and 1902 he showed that he could send a signal across the Atlantic although how it had got there he did not know. Others speculated that his signals were bouncing back to earth from a layer in the upper atmosphere, a theory that was proved correct much later.

These early days of commercial wireless were very exciting and my book concentrates on the period up to 1914 when all messages were sent in Morse Code. The most celebrated of these was the distress call from the Titanic in 1912 sent out by two young Marconi operators, only one of whom survived. The wireless rescue made Marconi an international hero.

"A fascinating story set in a fascinating period.."
Sunday Tribune

Further information from
info@backstory.la

www.backstory.la

backstory 🅱